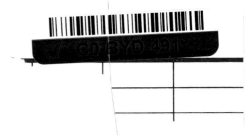

Democratic Practices in Education

Implications for Teacher Education

Edited by
Art Pearl and Caroline R. Pryor

Published in partnership with the
Association of Teacher Educators

Rowman & Littlefield Education
Lanham, Maryland • Toronto • Oxford
2005

Published in partnership with the
Association of Teacher Educators

Published in the United States of America
by Rowman & Littlefield Education
A Division of Rowman & Littlefield Publishers, Inc.
A wholly owned subsidiary of The Rowman & Littlefield Publishing Group, Inc.
4501 Forbes Boulevard, Suite 200, Lanham, Maryland 20706
www.rowmaneducation.com

PO Box 317
Oxford
OX2 9RU, UK

British Library Cataloguing in Publication Information Available

Library of Congress Cataloging-in-Publication Data

Democratic practices in education : implications for teacher education / edited
by Arthur Pearl, Caroline Pryor.
    p. cm.
    "Published in partnership with the Association of Teacher Educators."
    Includes bibliographical references and index.
    ISBN 1-57886-247-7 (pbk. : alk. paper)
    1. Democracy—Study and teaching—United States. 2. Teachers—Training
of—United States. I. Pearl, Arthur. II. Pryor, Caroline R. III. Association of
Teacher Educators.
    LC1091.D3964 2005
    370.11'5—dc22   2005002671

∞™ The paper used in this publication meets the minimum requirements of
American National Standard for Information Sciences—Permanence of
Paper for Printed Library Materials, ANSI/NISO Z39.48-1992.
Manufactured in the United States of America.

In memory of Ken Burdett and Kay Terry.
Although they passed away before the project was completed,
their leadership, collegiality, and dedication were vital to its completion.

Contents

Acknowledgments

Appreciation is extended to Dr. Tom McGowan, associate dean at the University of Nebraska, Lincoln, for his scholarship and support of Caroline Pryor's chapter in this book. We would also like to thank the board of directors of the Arizona Educational Research Organization (affiliate of AERA), who judged the fuller version of chapter 5 winner of the 1997/1998 best research paper.

Preface

In Defense of Democratic Education

Art Pearl, Washington State University, Vancouver, and Caroline R. Pryor, Southern Illinois University Edwardsville

> As one reads through the chapters of this volume, an underlying thread emerges. The thread throughout the discussion of democratic practices in education, regardless of whether we speak of public school grades K–12 or higher education, is that the students should have a voice in how things are done in that democratic classroom. (Terry, 1999)

The above was written by Kay Terry in her role as coeditor of this volume prior to her untimely death. Clearly, the mission of this book is to describe the importance of integrating tenets of democratic principles—liberty/ freedom, justice/fairness, equality/equal opportunity, inclusion, and the provision of a knowledge base sufficient to meet the responsibility of citizenship in an ever more complex world into our teaching. The contributors to this volume have explored various strategies and philosophies in support of this mission. At one level there is strong support for democratic education. At the very least there is recognition of its importance (Apple & Beane, 1995; Gutmann, 1987; Parker, 2002). However, at the level of classroom practice, that support withers and too often disappears. In recent years the teaching and implementation of democratic principles has not played a dominant role in the ongoing debate about the goals of American public education. While educators ponder whether test-based standards or a broad-based "liberal" education is the way to go (Anderson, 2002; Marshak, 2003), legislators resolve the debate by mandating accountability based on test-imposed standards.

The contributors herein offer their perspectives as insight into these controversies. They make their contributions, however, not as oppositional arguments, but as possibilities—the cumulative positive social effect of teaching from a democratic perspective.

The case made is for the importance of providing for education that promotes individual rights and develops the capacity to engage in collective action that respects those rights. These are two vital components of a democratic society. This book provides historical, epistemological, and practical responses to the question of the benefits of teaching about democratic principles. Bringing democratic education to the attention of educators and the general public is timely. Even the most ardent admirers of organizing schools around democratic principles wonder if this purpose is currently attractive to educators (Davis, 2003). Others wonder if educators are aware of the implications of not becoming a democratic practitioner (Kincheloe, 1999; Labaree, 1997).

Current educational priorities might not only block progress toward democratic practices; they could be inimical to democracy. Terry (1999) wrote, "Our schools are going in the opposite direction . . . to things [curriculum, testing, hiring] happening in and to schools and to the outside world [global uncertainty and unrest]" (p. 133). Terry's premise is that in a society that purports to support belief in democracy, democratic education is not central to the mission of public education. This book addresses this concern by presenting descriptions of programs or arguments that intentionally restore democracy into this debate.

If democratic principles are to become an integral part of public education, such understanding must be incorporated into teacher education programs. Given the now mandated standards-based models of education that preservice teachers observe in field-based preservice certification programs, is it desirable or even feasible for a university preservice program to teach democratic principles? The contributors to this volume present arguments and programs indicating that teacher educators are neither blind to nor ignorant of the leadership needed to provide for democratic education, each suggesting concepts and practices that serve, on reflection, as a reality base for democratic education.

Can preservice teacher education offer the attractiveness of domain-area method courses and field-based experiences in which components of democratic thought and critique have been purposefully interwoven? Caroline Pryor offers one such case. In a study in which democratic principles were integrated into a preservice to in-service teacher program, the intention to become a democratic practitioner rose significantly in the in-service stage (Pryor, under review). As a result of these findings, the university program entitled "Citizen Teacher" has begun a collection of resources and artifacts designed to enhance preservice teacher knowledge about how to implement democratic principles. One such artifact is Pryor's website, which contains a bibliography of K–6 books about democracy, annotated by the preservice teachers (http://tlac.coe.tamu.edu/faculty/courses/drpryor/books.pdf). A second resource is a workbook containing forms with questions about the use of democratic principles, designed for use in field observations (Pryor, 2000). Anecdotal evidence in favor of learning about purposeful reflection on democratic principles is compelling. One former preservice teacher reported the following:

> I do not have a classroom management problem. I use a town hall method with my students [first graders]. We choose the problems we want to discuss and then the class votes on what we should do. They have to decide what is fair [and just]. All the other teachers want to know what I do. I tell them, I am teaching them about democratic principles. This was pretty risky for me as a first year teacher. But it was also important. (student now teaching in Houston Independent School District)

Armando Laguardia and Arthur Pearl (chapter 2) and Armando Laguardia (chapter 4) bring to this book an understanding of democracy based on its fundamental principles. These principles provide a basis for both analysis and program implementation. One such principle is democratic authority as an argument against both authoritarianism and anarchy (Dahl, 1989; Ravitch & Thernstrom, 1992). The absence of concerted and informed challenges to arbitrary authority is particularly pernicious for preservice teachers because their lack of understanding of their power to teach about freedom or to model democratic authority has a cumulative effect on the continuance of freedom within a society. Rousseau, in his *Discourse on the Origin and Foundations of Inequality*, made freedom an inalienable human right (Ravitch & Thernstrom, 1992) that should be well understood. Laguardia and Pearl, in their chapters, draw from a much different tradition but reach a similar conclusion: one of the major purposes of education in a democratic society, certainly in our society, is to transmit an understanding of freedom as enunciated in the Bill of Rights, a cornerstone of democracy in the United States.

Numerous contributors to this book discuss the impact of preparing teachers to teach about democratic principles. Many also discuss the importance of applying democratic principles to teacher education. The logic here is quite clear; it is difficult to make a convincing case for democracy if you are unwilling to practice what you preach. Contributors call for an increasing student voice in teacher education programs—in both the management of the program and the course offerings. They call for respect for student rights and the demonstration of persuasive and negotiable authority. Central to these contributions is the need for K–12 educators to buy into the importance of teaching about human rights, dignity, and freedom and of becoming a "teacher-citizen" (Pryor, 2003), a leader who prepares other teachers to model and teach about the principles of democracy.

At one time it was understood that a primary purpose, if not the primary purpose, of public education was to prepare citizens. This is what George Washington implied in his farewell address:

> Promote then as an object of primary importance, institutions for the general diffusion of knowledge. In proportion as the structure of a government gives force to public opinion, it is essential that public opinion be enlightened. (Ravitch & Thernstrom, 1992, p. 139)

It is in reaching the goal of preparing democratic citizens that the limitations of current education policy and practices are most apparent:

> According to preliminary data from a U.S. Census survey conducted immediately after the 2000 election, 32.3 percent of all 18 to 24-year-olds voted in the 2000 elections, down from 32.4 percent in 1996—a record low turnout for this age group, says Peter Levine, deputy director of the Center for Information and Research on Civic Learning and Engagement (CIRCLE), which is affiliated with the University of Maryland.
>
> Census post-election surveys suggest that turnout among young adults in presidential years topped 40 percent as recently as 1992. In 1972, the first election in which 18-year-olds could vote, half of all 18 to 24-year-olds cast ballots.
>
> The anemic showing of young Americans at the polls in 2000 is particularly distressing because turnout overall increased to 54.7 percent from 54.2 percent in 1996, Levine says.

Even more ominous is the fact that the long-term decline in political participation among the young has occurred when other evidence suggests just
the opposite should be happening. (Morin, 2002, p. 24)

Ironically, as the need for informed citizens becomes acute, and as world
problems become more complex, those closest to educational institutions
are the most estranged from the political process. In the introduction we
ask if it is possible to have a democracy without democratic citizens. We
acknowledge that we are fast becoming such a society. Not voting is one
manifestation; another is not basing votes on reflected thought or reason.
Politicians no longer appeal to reason. Elections are reduced to entertain-
ment and the voters reduced to passive observers of a carefully crafted and
choreographed campaign organized to appeal to emotion and ignorance.
Media reinforces this corruptive process:

> Strategy coverage is marked by several features: (1) winning and losing as
> the central concern; (2) the language of wars, games, and competition; (3) a
> story with performers, critics, and audience (voters); (4) centrality of per-
> formance, style, and perception of the candidate; (5) heavy weighing of
> polls and the candidates standing in them. (Cappella & Jamieson, 1997,
> p. 33; Patterson [1993] makes an almost identical argument.)

How serious is the threat to democracy? And what implications do threats
to democracy have on education, particularly teacher education? These
questions are impossible to answer at present. There is no consensus. The
contributors to this volume certainly are not of one mind. Moreover, it is
difficult to reach a carefully developed conclusion while in the eye of a
hurricane. Perhaps Donald N. Wood overstates the case:

> The intellectual underpinnings of the developed world are crumbling—not
> just our schools and universities, but our entire institutional and philosoph-
> ical infrastructure. Our governmental systems, educational establishments,
> legal arrangements, economic and corporate organizations, and media struc-
> tures are all intellectual ideas. The political and economic foundations of the
> Great American Experiment were conceived as an intellectual outgrowth of
> the Enlightenment. But this intellectual legacy withers. This collapse of our
> intellectual heritage has resulted in our transition to a post-intellectual cul-
> ture. (Wood, 1996, p. 3)

We include this devastating conclusion, not necessarily because we find it convincing, but because we believe teacher educators do not have the luxury of underestimating the nature of the challenge. Reorganizing teacher education to create "teacher-citizens" capable of rousing students to informed citizenship responsibility is a prodigious task. It must begin with taking seriously the idea that the teacher should be a model citizen. Model citizenship has not been considered as part of teacher education admissions; nor are course or other experiences involved in the credentialing of teachers designed for such a goal. Teachers as citizens is a topic barely touched on by some of the contributors to this volume. It is an issue that needs much more discussion.

We also feel the need to examine another essential feature of democracy—inclusion. In one sense inclusion is the thrust of the reorganized Elementary and Secondary Education Act—now sloganized as "No Child Left Behind." But inclusion requires more than narrowing the test score gap, which seems to be the sole concern of the new legislation. Inclusion is important in every aspect of a democracy. As mentioned in the introduction, inclusion was very significant in the development of United States democracy. For all that progress and occasional retreats, inclusion in the form of access and equity continues to be an unmet democratic goal. There is a particularly important struggle for inclusion taking place in education involving exclusion from the teaching ranks. Here we find ourselves in yet another dilemma, one that Laguardia (in this book) probes in considerable depth. The achievement gap is not the only problem confronting education. There is also the demographic gap. As the student population becomes increasingly "minority"—that is, students of color who also happen to be disproportionately situated among the low academic achievers—the teaching ranks become increasingly "white." This is a condition that cries out for solution, but current recruitment strategies in education have not remedied this form of exclusion. The call for "upping the standards" for admission to teacher education that is so prevalent today might make inclusion even more difficult for currently underrepresented populations. Hopefully a serious reawakening of interest in democratic education will result in some fresh thinking and the opening of the door to those populations now excluded from teaching.

Democratic Practices in Education is an ambitious title for so slim a book. However, it accurately reflects the condition of education. Public schools have rarely accommodated democracy. Found here are toeholds, examples of some very preliminary actions and developing thoughts about democracy and its connection to teacher education. The intent is to stimulate a very necessary debate. If that debate results in democratic practices in education becoming much more the rule than the exception, we will have accomplished our mission.

REFERENCES

Anderson, L. (2002). Curricular alignment: A Re-examination. *Theory into Practice, 41*(4), 255–260.

Apple, M., & Beane, J. (1995). *Democratic schools*. Alexandria, VA: Association for Supervision and Curriculum Development.

Cappella, J. N., & Jamieson, K. H. (1997). *Spiral of cynicism: The press and the public good*. New York: Oxford University Press.

Dahl, R. A. (1989). *Democracy and its critics*. New Haven, CT: Yale University Press.

Davis, O. L. (2003). Does democracy in education still live? *Journal of Curriculum and Supervision, 19*(1), 1–4.

Gutmann, A. (1987). *Democratic education*. Princeton, NJ: Princeton.

Kincheloe, J. (1999). Critical democracy and education. In J. Henderson & K. Kesson (Eds.), *Understanding curriculum leadership* (pp. 70–83). New York: Teachers College Press.

Kincheloe, J. (2004). The knowledges of teacher education: Developing a critical complex epistemology. *Teacher Education Quarterly, 31*(1), 49–66.

Labaree, D. F. (1997). Public goods, private goods: The American struggle over educational goals. *American Educational Research Journal, 34*(1), 39–81.

Marshak, D. (2003, November). No child left behind: A foolish race into the past. *Phi Delta Kappan*, 229–231.

May, R. (1969). *Love and will*. New York: W. W. Norton.

Morin. R. (2002, January 14–20). A record low—and no one's cheering: A census survey shows that fewer young voters are going to the polls. *The Washington Post National Weekly Edition*, p. 24.

Parker, W. C. (2002). Teaching democracy: Unity and diversity in public life. New York: Teachers College Press.

Patterson, T. E. (1993). *Out of Order*. New York: Knopf.

Pryor, C. R. (2000). *Democratic classroom practice: Activities for the field experience*. Boston: McGraw-Hill.

Pryor, C. R. (2003). Teaching for democratic practice: Three strategies for the social studies methods course. *Teacher Education and Practice, 16*(2), 171–185.

Pryor, C. R. (under review). *Preservice to inservice changes in beliefs: A study of intention to become a democratic practitioner.*

Ravitch, D., & Thernstrom, A. (Eds.). (1992). *The democracy reader.* New York: Harper Perennial.

Terry, K. (1999). Democratic practices in education and curriculum. Chapter 8 draft in A. Pearl and C. Pryor, Eds., *Democratic Practices in Education.*

Wood, D. N. (1996). *Post-intellectualism and the decline of democracy: The failure of reason and responsibility in the twentieth century.* Westport, CT: Praeger.

Introduction

Art Pearl, Washington State University, Vancouver

Over the past decade there has been an increasing interest in democratic education, or, in the case of critical pedagogy, exposing its absence. There is no consensus on what democratic education means. Democracy is a protean concept. Unlike Mark Twain's weather, which "everyone talks about and nobody does anything about," democracy has everybody both talking and doing, although what they are talking about is difficult to decipher, their actions go off in all directions, and they claim as they go to epitomize democracy.

Democratic theorists are no more of one mind than practitioners in the field. It is a murky business, democracy, covering a wide range of issues and concerns. Democracy deals with the nature of authority, with inclusion into all facets of society, with knowledge required for responsible citizenship, with the nature of decision making, with rights of individuals, and with notions of equality. Different theorists emphasize different facets of democracy. Each component is viewed through a different lens, each theorist giving to it a different interpretation. And in this postmodern age what was already complicated becomes almost impenetrable.

None of the components of democracy, regardless of interpretation, come easy. That which was hard won rests on shaky ground. A cursory look at suffrage as one indication of inclusiveness can be instructive. The United States, now clearly the model of democracy throughout the world, has over its two hundred years of existence slowly granted more and more of its population suffrage. From a democracy modeled after ancient

Greece, it originally extended voting privileges to only property-owning males. Through spurts of intense organized effort of the excluded in alliance with small segments of the included, property restrictions, race restrictions, and gender restrictions on voting were eliminated. Most recently, with less struggle than characterized abolitionism and women's suffrage, the voting age was lowered from twenty-one to eighteen. Complicating the matter was the inclusion of immigrants as naturalized citizens. Some immigrants were treated much more favorably than others, and at times the country was swept with ferocious anti-immigrant bias. Overall, however, the record is clear. When it came to voting the United States has become increasingly inclusive. That is half the story.

The other half has to do with willingness to vote. Although more and more people in the United States can vote, fewer and fewer do. The last to be included, the eighteen- to twenty-one-year-olds, are the least likely to exercise what historically has been viewed as a precious right, important enough to die for.

This necessarily brings us to education. That portion of the population most closely connected to schools is the most disengaged. How much of this disengagement stems from undemocratic education is not presently known, but the alienation of youth from voting has to be a concern of all educators interested in democracy.

This book does not pretend to answer any of the large philosophical questions. A comprehensive and persuasive answer to these questions at this time is beyond the scope of this or any other work. We, instead, bite off a small chunk of the problem. What we attempt to do is consider a vital piece of the larger puzzle—teacher education as it affects some generally shared views of democratic practice in the classroom.

The contributors examine the relationship of teacher education and democratic practice from a variety of perspectives and accurately reflect the range of thinking and the diversity of emphasis on aspects of democracy as applied to teacher practices.

Jerry Ligon provides a solid foundation with a brief summary of current efforts to prepare students for democratic citizen responsibility in his chapter "Transforming Schools into Democratic Sites." He proposes a set of principles that would underlie democratic practices and describes two teacher education programs that applied those principles—a professional development school located at a middle school and a master of education field-based program. He stresses the importance of partnerships between the institutions of higher education and the elementary and secondary schools, the necessity of a democratic philosophy (John Dewey's and W. C. Parker's) informing the program, and teachers engaging in action research.

Armando Laguardia and Arthur Pearl elaborate the components of a democratic education in "Democratic Education: Goals, Principles, and Requirements." They make the case for a school authority as persuasive and negotiable and contrast such authority with democracy's two enemies—anarchy and guardianship. They identify and provide a response to various insidious forms of exclusiveness. Curriculum is recast as important problem solving. They specify particular student and teacher rights as inalienable. They call for the significant involvement of students in decisions that affect their lives and the responsibility of schools to provide students with what is necessary for the decisions to be based on logic and evidence. An important component in their conception of democracy is an optimum environment for learning. Laguardia and Pearl attempt to define the characteristics of such an environment. Lastly, they attempt to come to grips with the elusive concept of equality. Equality in education, to them, is equal encouragement obtained by equal access to the identified optimum environments for learning. Laguardia and Pearl believe that these concepts incorporated into a general theory provide a philosophical base for teacher education that will lead to democratic practices in elementary and secondary schools.

Paul Black makes the case for character education as an essential component of democratic teacher education in his chapter "Democratic Practices as Manifested through Character Education." Black provides a historical context drawing on the thoughts of Jefferson, Franklin, Horace Mann, and Dewey and, in the process, specifies the particular "character traits" whose development needs to be encouraged as part of democratic practices. These traits—for example, honesty, courage, respect, responsibility and justice—transcend ethic and cultural differences and have increasingly been included in state requirements.

In "Democracy, Schools, and Cultural Minority Groups," Armando Laguardia examines in considerable depth concepts of inclusion and equal encouragement that he (and Pearl) had introduced in the chapter on democratic goals, principles, and requirements. Laguardia begins with an international perspective and the impact that has led to massive migrations of populations and resulted in "inclusion, though not necessarily integration, of new racial, linguistic and ethnic communities" throughout the world. The United States has been the haven for immigrants from all over the world throughout its history. This has led to conflict in the schools never satisfactorily resolved by courts or by more overt political processes. Laguardia traces the historical developments and zeros in on the impact that a newly aroused conservative movement has had on education, putting enormous pressure on bilingual as well as multicultural education and adding impetus to the mounting drive for raised "standards as measured by standardized tests." He calls for a counterpolitical campaign in support of "access" and "equity."

Chapter 5, "European and American Influences on Democratic Practice at the Professional Development School: Postbaccalaureate Students in Early Field Experience" by Caroline Pryor, draws attention to the role of the teacher in society and the extent to which teachers perceive themselves as agents for a democratic society. Prefacing her chapter is a brief review of different perspectives on democracy that become the theoretical foundation for a specific field-based teacher preparation program. This particular program emphasized shared beliefs, reflected thinking, and support group meetings to deal with the "paradox of social integration and individual will." She makes a strong case for basing practice on articulated theory. Pryor advocates teacher education that brings student teachers and their mentors into collaborative activities. Such a program also encourages classroom teachers to become actively involved with reforming university-based teacher education.

Jeffrey Dunbar in "The Praxis of Democracy in Undergraduate Education" narrows his focus to a particular class—A Freshman Seminar, Ways of Knowing. The goals of the class included the development of "their dispositions, knowledge, and skills to engage some tangible academic, governance, or social reality that affected their college lives," and undertaking "democratic action to address that reality." The remainder of the chapter is a story in the voices of participating students that depicts an attempt to "overthrow the syllabus."

In a candid revelation, Fred Curtis, in "The Democratic Classroom: A Model That Works," describes how he came to appreciate the powerful positive effects of one aspect of democracy—meaningful participation in decisions that affect one's life. He came to the democratic classroom in a doctoral-level seminar when he was persuaded to restructure a class to conform to student interests. As a consequence his role as authority changed, and student investment and ownership increased. What happened as a result of a student proposal became established as ongoing practice with consistently satisfactory results.

In Chapter 8, "Democratic Practices in Education and Curriculum" by Kay W. Terry and Nancy P. Gallavan, Terry introduces the discussion of democracy by contrasting experiences in the United States with those during her visit to China and what was then the Soviet Union. Gallavan's experiences in her travels were similar. Both lament the excessive number of undemocratic classrooms in the United States. They conclude by presenting graduate student definitions of the attributes of democracy and explore various ways to introduce democracy in classroom choice, group work, inquiry and problem solving, student participation in important decisions, and ownership and how these can be part of teacher education.

The volume concludes with two different but logically connected discussions of democracy as shared decision making among stakeholders. Joseph Macaluso, in his chapter "Democracy in Education: Shared Governance," provides historical context and examines a shared-decision-making effort in a nonpublic elementary school. The program, although producing a pervasive "sense of commitment to change" and enhancing staff morale at all levels, unearthed difficulties that seriously undermined local efforts. The most serious obstacle to bottom-up democratic change is "steering from afar" in the form of ever-increasing mandates from state legislatures and state departments of education. He concludes that given the increased number of obstacles, it is imperative that teacher education take into consideration potential roadblocks and encourage risk taking in preservice and in-service programs.

John Bucci continues the argument for shared decision making in his chapter "Teacher Participation in School Decision Making." After briefly establishing the rationale for shared decision making he moves to the preparation of teachers for shared decision making and specifies the knowledge and skills needed by teachers for effective shared decision making. His is a pragmatic summation of all preceding contributions. He makes specific recommendations for an introductory course for persons aspiring to become teachers and for specific forms of skill training. He calls for schools of education to be models for shared decision making and to provide opportunities for student teachers to participate in such experiences and to include an emphasis on shared decision making in a variety of in-service professional development programs. Thus in a brisk, straightforward manner he brings to closure the loose ends that were necessarily a part of the wide-ranging discussions of the earlier contributions to the volume.

In summary, there is no more consensus about democracy among the contributors to this book than there is to be found anywhere else where democracy is seriously discussed. There are even incompatible notions about democracy given voice here, but that, too, can be instructive and constructive in the ongoing discussion linking education and democracy.

In the absence of consensus some very clear themes do emerge that all contributors promote and endorse. Democratic education, at the very least, is field based; is a partnership between higher education and elementary and secondary schools; is students, teachers, parents, and administrators involved in shared decision making; and is a determined and ceaseless commitment to equality.

Found here are serious reflections of persons with long and varied experience in teacher education. They share not only that experience with you but also a sense of what they have learned. If this small book can have any influence in moving schools of education in directions where there is agreement about a few vital requirements of democracy, it will have done very well indeed.

1

Transforming Schools into Democratic Sites

Jerry A. Ligon, National-Louis University

The idea of educating children for a democratic society is central to the rationale for public education in the United States. This rationale is typically found in "mission statements" and philosophies of education in schools. Unfortunately, it tends to stay there.

As a field of study or discipline, social studies is often "given" the responsibility of teaching young people the content, skills, and dispositions for democratic living: citizenship. The dominant approach to citizenship is cultural transmission focusing on content, loyalty, and patriotism. Instruction using prepackaged textbooks and rote acquisition, reliance upon teacher control and authority, and acceptance of existing or idealized social institutions (Goodlad, 1984; Shermis & Barth, 1982)—is an all too prevalent instructional routine in all subject areas.

Another dominant approach advocated by social studies theorists is reflective inquiry. This approach is based on active student learning, development of decision-making skills, and the use of social science knowledge to solve relevant problems or to understand issues. This approach has wide appeal in and out of social studies. Which subject area does not advocate active student learning?

Many subject areas call for decision-making skills and the use of inquiry to solve problems. One problem with this approach comes with "the selection of problems, the choice of relevant data and the conclusions, solutions or answers," that are usually provided for students by curriculum experts, text writers, and teachers (Shermis & Barth, 1982, pp. 31–32).

This safe selection of content leads to a classroom climate as emotionally flat as the dominant rote acquisition approach (Goodlad, 1984).

A third approach is democratic transformation. This approach rejects the views of cultural transmission and reflective inquiry because they maintain that democracy is a static quality rather than "a constant struggle for equality and justice." The democratic transformation approach advocates a classroom climate that engages students in the "processes of critical thinking, ethical decision making and social participation" (Stanley & Nelson, 1986, p. 532) in order to improve the quality of their lives and their communities (Goodman, 1992; Parker & Jarolimek, 1984; Parker & Kaltsounis, 1986; Wood, 1985). The democratic transformation approach is also an approach appropriate for all disciplines and fields of study. It is crucial, I believe, to have democratic practices and preparation for a democratic society as the goal of the entire school, all classrooms, and not only in the domain of the social studies department.

Therefore, democratic transformation should be infused throughout teacher education programs. In teacher education programs teacher candidates in foundation courses become acquainted with a nominal view of democracy often reflected in school district mission statements based on the ideas of Thomas Jefferson and Horace Mann: democracy requires educated voters.

Walter Parker (1996) reminds us of a stronger conception of democracy advocated by Dewey (1916/1985). Dewey understood that democracy involved more than a form of government, but a kind of living together: "a mode of associated living, of conjoint communicated experience" (p. 93). Precisely because our public schools are the place in our society where different interests and backgrounds come together, they are the sites—promising sites—for genuine civic apprenticeship.

Two excellent sources that describe already existing exemplary democratic practices in our public schools are George Wood's (1992) *Schools That Work* and Michael Apple and James Beane's (1995) *Democratic Schools*. They point out that the idea of democratic practice has been around for some time. It is not just the latest educational fad. They also stress the difficulty of implementing democratic practices; as Wood wrote, "nothing always works perfectly" (p. 5). Nevertheless, they demonstrate the possible, which, as Parker (1996) reminds us, "is their possibility" (p. 11). After all, schools can educate for authoritarianism just as easily, if not more easily, than they can educate for democracy.

I would like to suggest the beginning of a list of criteria or principles. Each should be considered in selecting exemplary skills, strategies, practices, and models that promote democratic practices.

- Faculty and staff should promote interaction of group members around numerous and varied interests that are consciously shared (Parker, 1996). This principle recognizes and builds on the fact that our schools are becoming—are—places where diverse children are gathered. They come with varied interests and cultural backgrounds. Schools, as public places, consciously need to build on those interests and promote interaction among diverse populations in schools.
- Schools should promote practices that recognize the use of "pedagogical authority" to ensure that interaction is wide ranging and unrestricted (Barber, 1992; Parker, 1996). A principle in a democratic society is that all have a right to be heard. In schools and classrooms it is essential that minority and unpopular opinions are expressed.
- Schools should focus on the public nature of education and promote the common good (Barber, 1992; Parker, 1996; Wood, 1992). Schools may be the last place in our society where people (at least young people) gather together and are involved in face-to-face interaction. In schools, young people from all parts of town, town and country, city and suburbs come together.
- Schools need to take advantage of their unique setting to promote understanding of diversity and the common good. Education should involve the "processes of critical thinking, ethical decision making and social participation" (Stanley & Nelson, 1986, p. 532) in order to improve the quality of students' lives and communities (Goodman, 1992; Parker & Jarolimek, 1984; Parker & Kaltsounis, 1986; Wood, 1985). Schools necessarily socialize. But instead of emphasizing socialization, democratic schools can lead "to civic empowerment and civic courage" (Kickbusch, 1987, p. 176).
- Schools that promote democratic transformation must reinterpret and reframe their practices to celebrate civic responsibility and human emancipation (to expand on Bartolome, 1994). No model or technique or curriculum package will work without our own critical reflection on our sociocultural histories, voices, experiences, and relationships.

WHAT MIGHT THIS LOOK LIKE?

A democratic teacher education program would need to look quite different from most of our current programs. A basic assumption of current, particularly undergraduate, programs is that the teacher candidate must "learn the tricks of the trade" or proceed through a carefully sequenced set of courses and experiences on the way to becoming a certified teacher. Then, graduate education is where practicing teachers refine and further develop their knowledge and skills to become master teachers. A democratic teacher education program would need to go beyond a preset teacher education curriculum, beyond what Bartolome (1994) calls the "methods fetish," where teachers put their faith in learning a strategy that will solve all their problems. Instead, teacher education must move toward a more open-ended education where the answers (and, indeed, the problems) are not necessarily known ahead of time.

To suggest the possibility of such a program, let me point to some promising areas by giving some examples from my own university experience with developing a professional development school and working in a master of education program that works with a cohort of practicing teachers.

PROFESSIONAL DEVELOPMENT SCHOOLS

The development of professional development schools is one of the most promising practices being developed today. Professional development schools allow universities and school districts to form partnerships for simultaneous renewal (Goodlad, 1997). While at Eastern Illinois University, I was involved in efforts to create a professional development school at the local middle school. The middle school was in the process of transforming itself from a junior high to a middle school. I arranged to have a section of a "general methods" course meet at the middle school and work with middle school faculty. A team of education professors in the College of Education offered assistance to the middle school and to me and my students. This section of the general methods course met for two periods (following the regular middle school schedule) every day at the middle school. During the first period I met with university students for purposes of instruction. Much of the time, a middle school teacher and I conducted the period together. The middle school teachers had agreed to work with my students and to have them participate in their classes during the following period of the day.

This way each middle school teacher and one or two university students were engaged over the length of a semester with the same students.

This arrangement made democratic practices possible. Middle school faculty, university faculty, and university College of Education students interacted as a group around the numerous and varied interests that are consciously shared by the middle school students. When a middle school student had a problem in understanding content or in classroom behavior, we all had a problem. We (middle school teacher, university professor, and teacher education student) discussed the problem, critically reflected on the situation, and discussed possible solutions to the problem. I worked to ensure that the interaction was wide ranging and that all were heard. This type of free and open discussion prevented any one person from proposing a solution to fit all situations—one method fits all. Instead, we worked together to reinterpret or reframe practices by listening to all voices, experiences, and relationships. In doing this, we created a community where we all learned from one another. I, as a university professor, learned much about the difficulties of putting theory into practice. The middle school teachers had to rethink many of their practices as they proposed and attempted to explain them to novice teacher education students. Finally, the teacher education students benefited from the exchange with "real" teachers and the university professor as they thought about and rethought about their experiences in a middle school.

I offer the professional development school as a possible site for democratic practices. If colleges of education and public schools can come together and associate in true partnerships with common education goals and a willingness to develop a community to work on shared difficulties, then democratic practices offer the possibility of reforming public schools and teacher education programs.

MASTER OF EDUCATION PROGRAM

I currently work in the M.Ed. field-based program at National-Louis University. The M.Ed field-based program is offered in the Interdisciplinary Studies program area. The curriculum is organized around four strands: group process/ human development and learning, curriculum and instruction, foundations/cross-cultural, and action research. An individual who enrolls in the program enrolls in eleven courses integrated over three terms for eighteen to twenty-two months. The teacher also becomes a part of a cohort of teachers assigned to one faculty member who facilitates the experience during the program (Burnaford & Hobson, 1995).

As a program that has its origins in progressive education, including the work of John Dewey and NLU founder Elizabeth Harrison, the "program seeks in its groups to create self-governing democratic communities that model learning, cooperation, and effective problem solving for the larger world and for the classrooms in which teachers are a part" (Interdisciplinary Studies Program, 1997). Our groups are made up of fifteen teachers, usually from roughly the same geographic area; often several teachers are from the same school or district. As a result, the teachers share many of the same problems and interests. As a progressive, student-centered program, we consciously build on those interests and promote interaction and group processes. Using the democratic principle that all have a right to be heard, the primary instructor facilitates the development of the group. Before long, a democratic community has been established that collaboratively plans the curriculum based on the curriculum of the program and the interests and needs of the particular group.

The curriculum experienced and made operational in the program is deliberated on with a democratic society that values diversity in mind. As Dewey reminded us, "The conception of education as a social process and function has no definite meaning until we define the kind of society we have in mind" (1916/1985, p. 103). This M.Ed. field-based program is concerned with issues of equity and social justice for all children (Interdisciplinary Studies Program, 1997). Schools and classrooms are not neutral places, and education is a moral enterprise. The Interdisciplinary Studies Program, by example, shows how democratic values can be enacted in a teacher education program.

One other aspect of the M.Ed. field-based program deserves mention. The research component of this program is a classroom-based action research project. This project directly involves the "processes of critical thinking, ethical decision making and social participation" advocated by Stanley and Nelson (1986). As action research it is done with an eye toward improving the quality of lives in the teacher's classroom. Teachers are encouraged to listen to their students through the lenses of qualitative research. Once teachers begin really listening to their students, they find they must reinterpret and reframe their practices, which leads teachers and their students to more liberating practices. Students are free, for example, to actually read in a reading program, rather than be drilled to death in mindless skills. Teachers are free to not spend endless hours marking and grading mindless worksheets, but rather to help children develop answers to their own felt needs and interests and learn more than the prescribed district curriculum dictates.

And, in some cases, this in-class teacher action research project leads to public action. One sixth grade class, for example, began with a simple canned food collection for a local charity at Thanksgiving, which developed into another project enabling students to develop a fuller understanding of international affairs and providing relief for a third-world country. One music teacher concerned about the effects of pencil and paper tests on his students was led to a project that questioned the assessment plan for music in the state of Missouri. As a result of this one teacher's action, the music arts assessment plan was changed.

CONCLUSION

What I hope these two examples taken from experiences in a professional development school and in a graduate teacher education program do is point to promising situations where democratic practices in teacher education programs are being and can be accomplished. This is an invitation for teacher education to embody the democratic qualities of associative living. Much is written about what the public schools (meaning K–12) should do and how they should be democratic. It is time for the colleges of education to take on an

> associationist vision of commonality where within and among these settings problems of common living are identified and mutual deliberation and problem-solving activity is undertaken as a routine practice of school life. (Parker, 1996, p. 12)

REFERENCES

Apple, M. W., & Beane, J. A. (1995). *Democratic schools*. Alexandria, VA: Association of Supervision and Curriculum Development.

Barber, B. R. (1992). *An aristocracy of everyone.* New York: Oxford University Press.

Bartolome, L. I. (1994). Beyond the methods fetish: Toward a humanizing pedagogy. *Harvard Educational Review, 64*, 173–194.

Burnaford, G., & Hobson, D. (1995). Beginning with the group: Collaboration as the cornerstone of graduate teacher education. *Action in Teacher Education, 17*(3), 67–75.

Dewey, J. (1916/1985). *Democracy and education: The middle works of John Dewey, 1899–1924* (Vol. 9). J. A. Boydston (Ed.). Carbondale: Southern Illinois University Press.

Goodlad, J. I. (1984). *A place called school.* New York: McGraw-Hill.

Goodman, J. (1992). *Elementary schooling for critical democracy.* New York: State University of New York.

Goodlad, J. I. (1997). Agenda for education in a democracy. *National Forum, 77*, 15–17.

Interdisciplinary Studies Program (1997). *Conceptual framework.* Wheeling, IL: National-Louis University.

Kickbusch, K. W. (1987). Civic education and preservice educators: Extending the boundaries of discourse. *Theory and Research in Social Education, 15*(3), 173–188.

Parker, W. C. (1996). *Educating the democratic mind.* Albany: State University of New York Press.

Parker, W. C., & Jarolimek, J. (1984). *Citizenship and the critical role of the social studies.* Washington, DC: National Council for the Social Studies.

Parker, W. C., & Kaltsounis, T. (1986). Citizenship and law-related education. In V.A. Atwood (Ed.), *Elementary school social studies: A research guide to practice* (pp. 14–33). Washington, DC: National Council for the Social Studies.

Stanley, W. B., & Nelson, J. L. (1986). Social education for social transformation. *Social Education, 50*(7), 528–530, 532–534.

Shermis, S. S., & Barth, J. L. (1982). Teaching for passive citizenship: A critique of philosophical assumptions. *Theory and Research in Social Education, 10*(4), 17–37.

Wood, G. H. (1985). Education for a democratic participation: Democratic values and the nuclear freeze campaign. *Theory and Research in Social Education, 12*(4), 39–56.

Wood, G. H. (1992). *Schools that work.* New York: Plume.

2

Democratic Education

Goals, Principles, and Requirements

Armando Laguardia and Art Pearl,
Washington State University, Vancouver

> Democracy is perhaps the most promiscuous word in the world of political affairs.
>
> —Bernard Crick, *In Defense of Politics* (1964, p. 18)

WHAT MAKES A DEMOCRATIC CLASSROOM DEMOCRATIC?

Any serious effort at facilitating democratic practice in schools would necessarily direct attention to the goals of a democratic education. Democratic practice in education addresses the following democratic themes or attributes: (1) persuasive and negotiable leadership, (2) inclusiveness, (3) knowledge made universally available and organized for important problem solving, (4) inalienable student and teacher rights, (5) universal participation in decisions that affect one's life, (6) the development of optimum learning conditions, and (7) equal encouragement. A review of these themes and attributes is an appropriate way to broaden one's understanding of democratic practices in schools.

Persuasive and Negotiable Leadership

One distinguishing feature of the democratic classroom is its leadership. The democratic authority, be it teacher, principal, superintendent, or board president, persuades and negotiates. Democratic leadership can be seen in sharp contrast to democracy's two major enemies, guardianship (authoritarianism) and anarchy (Dahl, 1989). Authoritarianism is the preferred mode of school authority in many instances. In many urban schools that serve the minority poor, student interests are neglected in a desperate tug-of-war between the authoritarian and the anarchistic.

Teacher education should not only adequately compare and contrast the different modes of authority but should also provide ample opportunity for prospective teachers to develop the requisite skills of persuasion and negotiation. Through the development of these skills democratic leadership can be nurtured.

Inclusiveness

A democracy establishes its legitimacy by its ability to draw all to it. Thus, democratic education is an alternative to the various forms of exclusion that have characterized schooling throughout its existence. Exclusiveness comes in many forms. It has been a major thread in educational policy throughout the twentieth century, manifest as ability grouping in elementary classrooms and as tracking in the high school (Oakes, 1985). Exclusiveness can be found in special education. The persistent call for heterogeneous groupings and the elimination of tracking and mainstreaming of special needs children in regular classrooms had been largely unsuccessful (or at best partially successful) because inclusiveness, in the absence of a general informing theory, is exceedingly difficult, if not impossible.

Exclusiveness is fostered by private schools and has been given impetus by recent efforts to privatize education through educational vouchers and by increasingly available charter schools.

The aim of these initiatives is to provide an escape from a public education system that has been unfairly savaged (see Berliner & Biddle, 1995). Escape from a public school system often means gravitation away from a necessary requirement of democracy—inclusiveness. Only when the perceived value of a general public school education is upgraded can such inclusiveness be achieved. The democratic strength of any society is determined by the quality of the education its most disadvantaged receive. Teacher education has a responsibility to thoroughly consider the issue of inclusiveness if democratic practice is to be more than an illusion.

Knowledge Made Universally Available and Organized for Important Problem Solving

Students go to school ostensibly to learn important things. But what constitutes important knowledge? Public discussion and debate over important knowledge is the important debate that has never happened.

Student opinion about what is important knowledge cannot be arbitrarily dismissed. Student desires for a better world, a fulfilling culture, an opportunity to engage in rewarding work, living harmoniously with self and neighbors, and preserving the environment are matters to be treated in depth in the curriculum. Refusal to adequately consider such issues results in students graduating from high school unprepared to deal with any important personal or social problems.

The issue of important knowledge impacts schooling in two ways. One involves the kinds and depth of knowledge taught, and the other determines which students get how much of it. These two issues are obviously connected. Little is to be gained if equality is achieved in useless, destructive, or trivial knowledge. Nor can democracy be sustained if knowledge is rationed by race, class, gender, or alleged capacity to learn. All students *need* that specific knowledge that can be used to solve what to them are important problems.

To argue that schools should not or cannot be involved in such education is to assume that some other agency will be involved, or that some benign elite can make fair and competent decisions in these vital areas. History provides ample evidence that neither is likely. Common social concerns need to be taught with centripetality in mind. Students must be encouraged, even exhorted, to common understanding. They need not and, on important problems, should not reach consensus. A major goal of teaching is to nurture in students the idea that decisions are made by informed majorities. The responsibility of those who find themselves in the minority is either to be persuaded by the majority argument or to accept the responsibility to continue to use accepted logic and rules of evidence to move enough others to their point of view to become the majority.

It is in this context that academic subjects are transformed from static tedium to vibrancy. Language is a means of communicating the important. Mathematics provides a way of thinking, a means of deciphering relationships and ordering evidence. Science is a process for accumulating evidence and determining lawfulness. History is a quest for solution. Through the arts individuals give expression to what they perceive to be important. The classics provide perspective. The basics are not educational ends, but means to ends that give day-to-day direction to Freire's 1970 advice that one should not only learn to read, but also read to learn.

When important knowledge is conceived as something that is democratically determined, every student is encouraged to evaluate, to weigh, to propose, to investigate, to debate. The student is less concerned with questioning authority than with becoming an authority. Students are liberated to the extent that they can make informed autonomous judgments on important issues.

It is conceivable, as many critics of education insist, that the goal of a curriculum as important problem solving made universally available is beyond the capacity of public schools as they are currently constructed. But until an effort is made to introduce important knowledge into the schools and teach it to all equally, we will never know what is possible. What we do know is that those who put ceilings on untested possibilities become enemies of youth and obstacles to solutions to problems regardless of what labels they attach to themselves.

In a democratic school, choice of career resides in the individual student, and the school fulfills its responsibility by providing accurate information about the complete gamut of careers, by discouraging premature foreclosure on choice, and by assuring all students that they have a right to consider any and all occupations. Even that would be insufficient. The encouragement of students to think about future occupations must be coupled with an in-depth study of economics to enable students to participate in economic planning and more specifically in policy decisions about employment development (a shared social concern). Education about employment must also bring the environment into the analysis to insure that economic plans do not come at the expense of livability. Individual choice melds with social responsibility in a democratic school.

A democratic decision process is used to determine the knowledge that is important for a democratic society. It is impossible to decree such knowledge. Knowledge in a democratic society is not spinach crammed down throats of resisting children for "their own good." Not everyone accepts the importance of certain knowledge, but everyone must be given the opportunity to be persuaded, to offer counterproposals, and to negotiate differences.

There is no magical formula to guide teachers in this debate over knowledge, but the more the teacher understands democracy, and the more that democracy is incorporated school-wide, the more likely the students are to accept the importance of what is taught. The guiding concept for a democratic plan of study is recognition that knowledge is neither handed to students as nonamendable commandments nor something that merely needs unfolding, but is, instead, a dynamic process involving everyone in debate leading to decisions made on the basis of accepted logic and evidence.

UNALIENABLE STUDENT AND TEACHER RIGHTS

Individual rights are the foundation on which democracy is built. Without them there is no beginning, no place to stand. The determination of appropriate knowledge and the quality of participation depends on the rights that each individual possesses as (to use Tawney's words) "practical powers" (Tawney, 1964). Currently, students have few rights, and even those that they have are unequally bestowed and unevenly respected. Students are often taught about rights the very moment they are denied them.

Defining Rights

What precisely is a right? There are many definitions—none definitive. We find a rather restrictive definition most useful in sustaining democratic practice in classrooms. Our definition follows: a right is an unabridged activity that does not restrict the activity of others or require from others some special effort (e.g., the payment of a tax to provide another with subsistence). Freedom of expression under this definition is a right because one person's expression does not prevent another from also expressing him- or herself. Respecting one person's privacy does not invade another's privacy. Due process for one does not come at the expense of the due process for another. One's freedom of movement does not restrict another's freedom of movement.

Rights, by this definition, must be extremely few. These few must be fully understood and scrupulously protected. Here, rights are considered from two perspectives: one, as an important curriculum issue, and two, as a means by which the nature of the relationship between adult authority and students (as well as administration and teachers) is defined. What troubles us is the extent to which current school practices and curriculum foster contempt for the underpinnings of our cultural and legal definitions of democracy, regardless of how rights are defined.

Rights, like all of democracy, are not simple. Each right has a fuzzy boundary and can be rescinded in states of emergency. The gray areas and conditions of emergency are important areas of the negotiations that become the practiced curriculum in the classroom. In democratic education student rights should derive from the United States Bill of Rights.

Our call for student rights is simple and straightforward and should be self-evident. In the democratic classroom students should have only the rights that are the entitlements of all citizens.

In a democratic classroom students have the rights they are born with, and they learn to be responsible. In the authoritarian classroom responsibility is a prerequisite for rights. Only the responsible are allowed rights. In anarchy, anything can be claimed as a right. The rights-responsibilities relationship is an important subject of debate that needs to be brought into the classroom. Teachers teach rights by both analyzing and practicing them. We limit our discussion to four rights, not because these are all there should be in a democratic society, or even all that have been discussed, but because these four constitute a basic minimum that have successfully withstood the test of time. The four are (1) rights of expression, (2) rights of privacy, (3) rights to a particular form of due process, and (4) rights of movement.

Rights of Expression

In the United States these are commonly referred to as the "First Amendment rights." The "founding fathers," despite limited experience in democracy and their lack of commitment to important democratic principles, understood that there was no protection whatsoever against an authoritarian resurgence unless freedom of speech, press, worship, and assembly were guaranteed to all those deemed citizens. Would that school authorities were so enlightened. Rights currently are taught as meaningless abstractions, so ill defined that students are unable to distinguish between rights and perversions of them. Freedom of speech should be the right to express an unpopular opinion and to disagree with established authority. The right does not extend to slander, to racial epithets, or to the disruption of others while they are exercising their rights of expression. It does not require others to listen. In fact requiring others to pay attention is a violation of another precious right not respected in school, the right not to be a captive audience.

Student rights of expression in a democratic classroom. Students must be encouraged to state opinions. It is essential that criticism of adult authority, teachers, or administration not be suppressed. Such criticism can and should be answered by adult authority, not squelched by it. It is an imperative that students in no way be threatened or punished for disagreeing with the adult authority. Ridiculing students or otherwise exploiting the advantage of position that a teacher has is suppression of a right. In a democratic classroom, student newspapers are not censored (although the United States Supreme Court has ruled that school officials can censor). Students' rights to petition and to assemble are also respected in the democratic classroom. In fact, free speech areas, as well as opportunities to debate significant issues, should be created in every school.

Is conversing in a language other than English covered by rights of expression? The language a person uses does more than communicate information to others. Language also expresses identity and loyalty. All oppressed people develop secret codes that they use to communicate to those they trust and keep those they do not trust in the dark. That is why so many adolescents speak in a language their parents and other older individuals cannot understand. Any in-school effort to suppress the language spoken at home should be seen as a violation of a student's rights of expression. To be democratic, teachers and other officials need to find persuasive reasons for students to become fluent in English. If students resist learning English, school officials should look for oppressive conditions that lessen the desire for students to learn English.

Rights of Privacy

> Blanket searches of school children are not part of any traditional school function of which I am aware.
> —Supreme Court Justice Sandra Day O'Connor, 1995 (Quoted by Trebach & Ehlers, 1996, p.15)

Democracy guarantees its citizens a private life. Privacy is threatened by both a lack of understanding of its importance and the increased technical capacity to pry. School authorities find many excuses to intrude into students' lives. Concern about drug use or possession of other contraband has been deemed sufficient to mandate student submission to drug testing and to searches of lockers or persons. Respecting the right to privacy is difficult. School authorities must act decisively if the health and safety of students are threatened. There are, with privacy, as with all rights, situations that justify abrogation, but the issue in schools is to publicly acknowledge the student's right to privacy, the unusual circumstances where violation of that right is justified, and the assurance that the privacy right of every student will be equally protected. The challenge is to find ways to protect the general public without undermining rights. This requires that much more attention be given to other requirements of democracy. It is easier to respect the rights of privacy if students participate in the decision-making processes that lead to the establishment of rules. Rights of privacy are also easier to protect if students have available to them more complete knowledge of a problem to be solved and a more thorough understanding of the arguments defending the different proposed solutions to that problem. The student concern for privacy includes the right to personal life, security of one's lockers or desks against unreasonable searches and seizures, and protection of confidentiality, for example, recognition of the privacy of assessment, students' personal records, and students' problems in school.

Due Process

The Constitution of the United States in Amendments IV through VIII defines a system of due process. These amendments need to be understood and practiced in schools. The due process protection in the Bill of Rights defines the parameters of school discipline policy and practice. Due process rights should be taught respectfully.

All of the due process amendments in the Constitution are designed for one goal—the establishment of a system of "fairness." While the founding fathers did not support democracy or equality in general, there was one area where equality was very important to them, and that was equal treatment before the law. Distrustful as they were of democracy and universal suffrage, and as committed as they were to class hierarchy, they were also firm believers in fairness—the same justice system applied equally to all regardless of social standing (slaves excepted and women also given short shrift). Even that limited notion of fairness has been difficult to achieve and will not be achieved unless more attention is given to creating a fair due process system in schools as preparation for the responsibilities of citizenship.

It is the lack of perceived fairness or guarantees of fairness in schools that produces so much alienation and anger. Students complain long and loud across time and space about the unfairness of discipline. These complaints are not taken seriously. As a consequence, students experience twelve years of schooling without any serious opportunity to appreciate the reasoning behind the logic for limitation of police powers that are found in the Bill of Rights.

Rights of Movement

Here schools are in a quandary. Attendance in school is compulsory. And yet fundamental to democracy and to the notion of human rights is freedom of movement. There are many arguments supportive of compulsory education, some of which we find persuasive, but compulsory education does not necessarily mean that student movement must be as restricted as it currently is, nor does it mean that students must be captive audiences. Rights are not easily transferred into practical powers, but schools can function efficiently while respecting rights of movement.

One reasonable approach to democratizing compulsory education is to increase the number of choices that students have in school. No student should be required to remain in a situation that he or she does not find gratifying (and certainly in none found intolerable). Students should be able to exercise choice in teachers, classes, and schools. Students' charges of unfair treatment have to be taken seriously. Choice can be very difficult for schools. Some classes, schools, and teachers are much more popular than others. But the difficult is not impossible. If, on the basis of increased choice, some classes and some schools become undersubscribed—that is, very few students want to be there—it is incumbent on the school system to take necessary action either to change the classes or school or to find ways to persuade students to want to be there.

In schools today rights are rarely taught and even more rarely practiced. For rights to be real, teachers must understand them both in theory and as they have been practiced throughout the years. Teaching rights means both granting them and reflecting on them. Teachers who have had little involvement in the understanding and the practicing of rights are not likely to teach them with much conviction.

UNIVERSAL PARTICIPATION IN DECISIONS THAT AFFECT ONE'S LIFE

> Democratic solutions will emerge only from the trial-and-error of active citizens who learn for themselves how to do politics, who discover the methods and principles that work because people have tried and occasionally failed. It requires of people the patience to accumulate social understandings that they have tested against reality and then to pass on their knowledge freely to others. Strange as it may seem to an era governed by mass-market politics, democracy begins in human conversation. (Greider, 1992, p. 41)

The classroom is the place for exactly that kind of conversation, and because almost all children and adolescents go to a public school, if the interactions are allowed to take place and be meaningful, there will be important talk across all kinds of differences. "When the circle is enlarged to include others, they will be embarking on the fertile terrain of politics that now seems so barren (Greider, 1992. p. 41).

Democracy makes demands on its citizens. They are responsible for their government, for the husbanding of natural resources, for maintaining standards of civility, for the policies that "fine tune" the economy, and for establishing the conditions for interpersonal relationships. If they do not accept this responsibility, they are at the mercy of others. When George Bernard Shaw (1903) condemns democracy as the rule of the incompetent many replacing the corrupt few, he criticizes not democracy but the inadequate preparation for democratic citizenship. Self-government requires two kinds of knowledge. The first supplies the evidence that is applied to social and personal problems. The second knowledge is of process— learning how to work with others to arrive at decisions. Schools concerned about democracy assume a measure of responsibility for both of these forms of knowledge. Effective participation requires the mastering of certain democratic arts or skills that include the ability to marshal a persuasive argument, the willingness to listen and understand the arguments of others, the capacity to negotiate, the willingness to work cooperatively with a wide range of others, the ability to assume leadership and the willingness to relinquish it, and the capacity to establish goals and to evaluate progress to those goals. The following are necessary if a student is to become an effective and responsible citizen: (1) a revitalized school government, the most important unit of which is the classroom; (2) participation in cooperative learning activities informed by democratic principles; and (3) involvement with meaningful community service.

Student participation in meaningful decision making does not imply surrendering authority to students. Teachers remain in control. Inviting students to participate in decisions does not undermine leadership; it enhances it. An adversary teacher-student relationship is replaced by a system of mutual respect and accountability. Involving students means precisely that. The teacher no longer attempts to be the supreme authority (a role impossible to play and a contributing factor in school disruption) and becomes instead a legitimate authority who explains and defends decisions while encouraging students to make suggestions that will be considered seriously. The process of participation must proceed rationally and developmentally. As students grow older, they should take on more and more responsibility. Here again we confront an idiosyncratic school system. There is no perceptible logic in the ways students currently participate in decisions in school. Very young children are consulted and choice is made in a manner that is hardly democratic but is much more so than what happens a few years later. The older the students get, the less power they have in school (Lewis, Lovegrove, & Burman, 1991). As students grow and are enrolled in schools with much larger numbers of students, they are increasingly perceived as potential threats, and the school adopts policies to further limit student power to make decisions.

Social background correlates highly with current student participation in decision making. Advantaged students participate; students from deprived backgrounds and with undistinguished academic records do not. Limiting participation is an important factor in the social reproduction of privilege and privation that a democratic education struggles against.

Not all participation, even that which purports to be democratic, is educational. There are games played with participation. Students participate in trivial decisions while adult authorities make the important ones. The effect of this charade is to reinforce the idea that only a certain few have the capacity to decide on vital issues. It is the treatment of students as objects to be manipulated as much as the meaninglessness of the material to be mastered that feeds authoritarianism and produces cynicism. Both manipulation and meaningless subject material are addressed in education designed to preserve and extend democracy. Learning to be a democratic participant is engaging in a democratic means to a defensible end. Participation that does not attain the goal must be critically reviewed. Teachers and other educational leaders have the responsibility to draw attention to the failures to reach goals and to suggest better ways of participating. Failure to attain a goal should never be used as an excuse to eliminate democratic participation in favor of authoritarian control. The proper response of school authorities for breakdowns in the participation in working toward a goal is guided reflection on the participation, proposed alternatives, renewed debate about these alternatives, and, through this participatory process, the arrival at new plans.

The critical test of democracy is whether it is possible for citizenship skills to be broadly and evenly distributed. That is also the test of the democratic classroom. It is in the exercise of power that persuasiveness is tested.

THE CREATION OF AN OPTIMUM
ENVIRONMENT FOR LEARNING

Only a democratic classroom has the capacity to create optimum conditions for learning for *everyone*. That is the great advantage democracy has over its two enemies, guardianship and anarchy. Guardianship restricts growth, and anarchy limits the benefits of positive leadership. However, optimum conditions cannot be created unless first defined. Research in human motivation and educational climate as well as our own experiences over three decades have led us to the following ten attributes of an optimum learning environment: (1) encouragement to risk, (2) relief from unnecessary pain, (3) meaning, (4) sense of competence, (5) belonging, (6) usefulness, (7) hope, (8) excitement, (9) creativity, and (10) ownership.

Encouragement to risk. For risk taking to be encouraged the teacher must achieve a balance between challenge and support. In existing classrooms inequality is based not on encouragement to risk but rather on active and persistent differential *discouragement* to risk. Very early in school life many students learn that they should not risk because the costs of risking far outweigh any benefits. *Unwillingness* to risk distinguishes the nonachiever from the achiever. We believe that unwillingness to risk is less a personality attribute than it is part of the social environment. Teachers communicate clearly who will be punished for risking and who will not. Students who have been fearful, insecure, and school failures can blossom when encouraged to risk (Hollins, 1991; Meier, 1995).

Relief from Unnecessary Pain. For most students, school is an uncomfortable place. Students find most "subjects" deadening and school "boring" (Goodlad, 1990). Boring as school is in general it is far more intensely so for those assigned to the lower tracks (Goodlad, 1990, p. 155). It is not merely student opinion that low-track classes are more uncomfortable than college-bound tracks. Independent observation provides verification of dreary curriculum and instruction (Oakes, 1984; 1992). It is impossible to make schools universally entertaining. That is not a realizable or even a desirable goal. What can and should be eliminated is unnecessary pain. In school, unnecessary pain takes the form of humiliation, shame, boredom, imposed silence, and loneliness. Teachers and administrators are not the only ones who inflict unnecessary pain. Students do it to each other. Bullying, harassment, and name-calling are all part of the existing "at-risk" school culture. However, the fact that students inflict pain on other students does not absolve the teacher from altering that situation. Drawing attention to the process, generating projects that address the situation, actively engaging in team building, counseling individuals, continuously consulting with students and keeping a record of hours, days, and weeks without putdowns, and so on, all help develop a new culture.

Meaning. Meaning is insufficiently understood in our society. Meaning in school has two fundamentally different *meanings*. In one of its senses, students need to understand what is expected of them in any class activity, and in the other, students need to know that what they are learning is important. In today's classroom there is wide discrepancy in communicating both senses of meaning. Because of the way meaning is treated and because of the remote and arcane methods used to evaluate student performance, students are often so confused that they are no longer able to ascertain for themselves what they know. They have lost ownership of their intelligence and thus are unable to determine if they can or cannot read, multiply, or analyze a historical situation. In a democratic classroom all students receive equal justifications for the lesson and are equally enlightened as to how the lesson is to be learned. In the democratic classroom students assist the instructor in demystification, enlightening each other regarding what is to be done. (See Corbett & Wilson, 1998, for students' assessment of the importance of making instructions clear and how rarely that occurs.)

Sense of competence. Developing in students a sense of their own competence is a vital condition of an optimum learning environment (White, 1959). Currently only a select few are so encouraged to develop that sense. Those who are not so encouraged learn quickly who they are and in time begin to perceive themselves as teachers perceive them (Wigfield, Eccles, & Rodriguez, 1998). For an optimum learning environment, it is necessary for teachers to encourage in all a sense of competence. In school, competence and relevance are inseparable. It is difficult to encourage students to be competent in matters that they find insignificant. Students are far more likely to strive to be competent when the knowledge and skill they are developing are organized for important problem solving.

Belonging. Ours is a society that systematically includes and excludes. In an earlier time family, neighborhood, union, church, and fraternal order provided psychological centering and opportunity for psychological investment. Such a society was inequitable and blatantly unfair, but it provided gratifications, many of which have been lost. The "existential vacuum" noticed by so many is partially the result of the technological takeover of community. Passive reception has replaced active participation. So much of today's life is centrifugal and impersonal. Belonging is a vital human need. Humans hunger for companionship. They are terrified by isolation. Schools have always included and excluded. Exclusion from welcomed membership in school does not terminate a student's desire for belonging. Students demeaned, humiliated, and excluded from first-class membership in school, that is, those with attributed "deficits," will search for belonging outside of school-sanctioned activities. They will join cliques, gangs, and so on, to establish identity, and they will demonstrate affiliation by dress, music, language, designation of "turf," identifying behaviors (which can include violence), shared values, and other indicators of a "common culture" (Willis, 1990). These groups become references for acceptable and unacceptable behavior and in time rob established authority of its legitimacy. An optimum learning environment is one that welcomes every student as an equally important member of a learning community, one in which all students are encouraged to be part of the effort to make the classroom an inclusive community. Welcoming all students equally not only makes a community out of the classroom but also prepares students for community building in the broader community. It is one antidote to racism, ethnocentrism, sexism, and homophobia.

Usefulness. Uselessness is a dreaded condition. Enforced uselessness is cruel punishment, and yet enforced uselessness is the essence of existing classrooms. The raison d'être of current education is preparation for *future* usefulness. And that is one of the reasons students find school so deadly. They are asked to put their lives on hold. In our formulation of democratic education schools prepare students for future challenges, but at the same time usefulness is built into day-to-day classroom activity to achieve an optimum learning environment. Usefulness is perceived as a developmental attribute. The skills, insights, and knowledge obtained in the process of being useful in school provide the basis for continual growth that opens doors to a variety of valuable paid and volunteer adult experiences of usefulness. Usefulness in school is achieved when all students are given a wide range of choices in providing services to others and also a wide range of choices in accepting the services of others. Usefulness in school is meaningful problem solving rather than mindless drill and alleged preparation for a dubious and murky future. In an optimum learning environment *all* activities are organized for usefulness. The problems students solve are problems students perceive to be real and important. All students are recruited to help with the instruction and serve in many different capacities. All engage in cross-age tutoring, all share the results of research with the class, and all have valuable roles to play in cooperative education projects. All engage in community service that is integrated with the basic curriculum and have comparable responsibility and equal choice as to the nature of that community service.

Hope. "It is because modern education is so seldom inspired by a great hope that it so seldom achieves a great result. The wish to preserve the past rather than the hope of creating the future dominates the minds of those who control the teaching of the young" (Russell, 1927, p. 110). A few decades ago, at least in the United States, it would have been unnecessary to include hope as an unmet human need. It sprang eternal; it was the essence of our national character and was manifest everywhere. We largely believed with Franklin Roosevelt that "the only thing we had to fear was fear itself." Hopelessness now comes at us from many sources. Pessimism is reflected in opinion polls and loss of confidence in one's ability to influence one's future (Morin, 1995). Pessimism is the one common characteristic in modern American life—although times are good, middle class and poor, black and white alike fear the American dream is not for them. If an optimum learning environment is to be achieved, a serious effort must be made to equally encourage all students to be hopeful. However, inspiring hopefulness cannot degenerate into cheerleading. An optimum learning environment can be achieved only when all students are provided powerful *reasons* to be hopeful. Such optimism is the result of continuous dialogue. Problems are organized with possible solutions in mind. And students are encouraged to be problem solvers rather than be overwhelmed by the problems they have.

Excitement. Excitement is a legitimate and important human need. Excitement is not a term that students usually associate with classrooms unless there is a fight or someone lights a fire in the wastebasket. But there are rare moments, treasured and forever relived by a few successful students who are able to experience the intense feelings of fulfillment that come with discovery, invention, and creativity. What is rare should be the norm. All students, rather than a privileged few, should be excited by what goes on in a classroom. When the classroom is not an exciting place, some students try to make it so. It is not the "good" students who bring excitement to the class, but the "bad" ones. The troublemakers create their own excitement and share it with the rest of the class. They engage in outrageous, that is, exciting, action because they believe they have nothing to lose. It is one of the few times students with a stake in the system, if they do not envy the "bad" students, certainly enjoy their presence. Excitement is another characteristic of an optimum learning environment. Excitement is almost always not an attribute of the authoritarian classroom. Most school-based "excitement" is relegated to athletics and other cocurricular activities such as opening night of the carefully selected school play, and as such it is restricted to a few carefully screened students. Classrooms can be designed to be exciting only if teachers are willing to relinquish control and students are encouraged to participate in activities where they generate important knowledge, make important discoveries, and partici-pate in important decisions. For the classroom to be democratic, the op-portunity for such excitement is consciously extended to all students, and when it is apparent that some students find the classroom more exciting than others, the situation is discussed in class, and efforts are made to ex-tend excitement to all.

Creativity. Humans are, by nature, a creative species. Each generation creates a new world. School officials, with a logic similar to that used for assessing intelligence, arbitrarily establish limits on creativity, insisting that only a privileged few are creative. Creativity is in a certain sense undefin-able. There are no acceptable criteria for creativity, and often it goes un-recognized. Creativity should not be defined solely by school-recognized accomplishment, or by an even more capricious criterion-assessed capac-ity to be creative. In an optimum learning environment all students are en-couraged to be constructively creative and to use creativity for community building, that is, to make the class a far more interesting, exciting, and creative place than is currently the case. The democratic classroom un-leashes the imagination of all students.

Ownership. In an optimum learning environment students own their intellectual product. They do things for themselves and for their commu-nity and not for established authority. Students are far more motivated to achieve when they believe that they have a stake in the educational activ-ity. There is powerful evidence indicating that students are motivated to invest in education when they "own" their schoolwork.

EQUALITY

Perhaps the ultimate test of any society is its ability to be fair. Fairness is a salient issue in the United States. Here and elsewhere, various minori-ties, women, the handicapped, the aged, and gays and lesbians have launched campaigns to eradicate bias and less than equal treatment in the workplace, schools, the courts, and public accommodations. Despite all of these efforts the world remains unequal, and the gains made have been painfully slow, often reversible and, all too often, illusory. To fully grasp the problem it is important to recognize that in recent years the relation-ship between school and work has changed dramatically. The society that is emerging increasingly relies on school achievement as a prerequisite for entry into status positions, and, thus, the school has become the principal institution regulating status flow. We have become a credential society.

Credentials are the visas into desirable work. Because of its responsibility for credentials, the school directs students either to desired or to less than desirable careers with virtually no knowledge of how well they are suited for such activity. The judgments made are gratuitous and reproduce existing social hierarchies (Bowles & Gintis, 1976).

One way to look at equal encouragement is to more critically examine what happens to students in classrooms. Is success a function of individual capabilities, or is it the result of systemic or teacher actions that encourage some and discourage others? The educational establishment has limited debate about student performance almost exclusively to individual differences. School failure or disruption is attributed to student "deficits." Over the years fierce debate has raged between those who see the deficits as inherited (Burt, 1972; Herrnstein & Murray, 1994; Jensen, 1969) and those who perceive the deficits as stemming from "accumulated environmental deficits" (Deutsch, 1967; Hunt, 1961), and those who posit inadequate socialization as the cause for school failure (Aichhorn, 1983; Moynihan, 1965), and cultural deficit theorists who insist that specific cultures militate against academic success (Lewis, 1961; Miller, 1958).

The pervasiveness and the protean nature of deficit thinking as it applies to students of color, women, and the poor in general are treated in depth by Valencia (1997). What has emerged is a consensus that certain minorities and the traditionally poor are in some way inferior; the debate is only over etiology. The issue has been studied, and the scientifically unchallengeable conclusion reached, to whit, is ours is an essentially fair society, the cream has risen to the top, and they who got there, got there legitimately. The role that the school plays in generating inequality is minimized, if not dismissed. (The revision of the Elementary and Secondary Education Act, No Child Left Behind, does hold the school accountable and demands that schools end the achievement gap within a decade, not by making schools more democratic, but by making them less so. Unlike leftist criticisms of schools that blame failure of poor and otherwise marginalized students on the oppressiveness of racism, classism, sexism, and homophobia [See, e.g., Giroux, 1988a, 1988b, 1997; McLaren, 1986, 1995, 1997, 1998], now the blame is attached to permissiveness, teacher unions [categorized by Secretary of Education Paige as "terrorists"], school bureaucracy, and the "socialism" of public schools. The carefully orchestrated attack on public schools, culminating in high-stakes testing systems imposed state by state and further legitimated under a nationally imposed No Child Left Behind umbrella, is a far cry from dealing with specific grievances of students and parents in a particular classroom or school. If anything the hysteria created in schools by No Child Left Behind [and other high-stakes testing initiatives], pushes individual grievances even further into the background.)

One area of potential inequity that has received some attention is the separation of students into different learning tracks (Oakes, 1985). We have long opposed tracking, but it may not be the most virulent form of unequal treatment in schools. Teachers differentially encouraging and discouraging student success within a classroom is more insidious and might be more important in influencing student academic performance.

This encouragement and discouragement takes the form of systematic denial of students' access to optimum learning environments. This denial or unequal availability of an optimum learning environment becomes, in time, reified into distinct school cultures that are institutionalized by practice, policy, and statute.

What happens with equal encouragement? A number of wide-ranging studies have shown that equal encouragement not only narrows the differences between the "able," "competent," and "gifted" and those with attributed deficits but can completely eliminate those differences (Hollins, 1991: CBS Film, *Love Mary*, 1985; Pearl, 1972).

There are many ways to come to democratic education. The ideas presented here derive from over thirty years of experience and experimentation in democratic education. This chapter is coauthored by two who were involved in a democratic education experiment over thirty years ago. One was an "at-risk" student, brought to the University of Oregon as an inadmissible student to test whether admission requirement were "standards" or barriers. That once inadmissible student has a doctorate and is on the faculty of Washington State University, having spent the better part of the last thirty years as a student, an administrator, and a designer and evaluator of programs for at-risk youth. The other continues to learn what democratic education is from his students and his political relationships in the community. It is out of these experiences that a general theory of democratic education has emerged. They present it as an invitation for a long overdue debate.

28 *Democratic Education*

REFERENCES

Aichhorn, A. (1983). *Wayward youth*. Evanston, IL: Northwestern University Press. (First published in 1925 as *Verwahrloste Jugend*. Vienna. Internationaler Psychoanalytischer Verlag.)

Berliner, D. C., & Biddle, B. J. (1995). *The manufactured crisis: Myths, fraud, and the attack on America's public schools*. Reading, MS: Addison-Wesley.

Bowles, S., & Gintis, H. (1976). *Schooling in capitalist America: Educational reform and the contradictions of economic life*. New York: Basic Books.

Burt, C. (1972). The inheritance of general intelligence. *American Psychology, 27*, 175–190.

Corbett, H. D., & Wilson, B. L. (1998). Scaling within rather than scaling up: Implications from students' experiences in reforming urban middle schools. *The Urban Review, 30*(4), 261–293.

CBS Film. (1985). *Love Mary*.

Crick, B. (1964). *In defence of politics*. Harmondsworth, UK: Penguin Books.

Dahl, R. A. (1989). *Democracy and Its Critics*. New Haven, CT: Yale University Press.

Deutsch, M. (1967). *The disadvantaged child*. New York: Basic Books.

Edmonds, R. (1984). School effects and teacher effects. *Social Policy, 15*(2), 37–40.

Friedenberg, E. Z. (1959). *The vanishing adolescent*. Boston: Beacon Press.

Freire, P. (1970). Pedagogy of the oppressed. (M. B. Ramos, trans.) New York: Seabury Press.

Giroux, H. A. (1981). *Ideology, culture and the process of schooling*. Philadelphia: Temple University Press.

Giroux, H. A. (1983). *Theory and resistance in education: A pedagogy for the opposition*. South Hadley, MA: Bergin and Garvey Publishers.

Giroux, H. A. (1988a). *Schooling for democracy*. London: Routledge & Kegan Paul.

Giroux, H. A. (1988b). *Teachers as intellectuals*. Granby, MA: Bergin & Garvey Publishers.

Giroux, H. A. (1997). *Pedagogy and the politics of hope: Theory, culture, and schooling*. Boulder, CO: Westview Press.

Good, T. L., & Brophy, J. E. (1991). *Looking in classrooms* (5th ed.). New York: Harper and Row.

Goodlad, J. L. (1990). *Teachers for our nation's schools*. San Francisco: Jossey-Bass Publishers.

Greider, W. (1992). *Who will tell the people: The betrayal of American democracy*. New York: Simon & Schuster.

Herrnstein, R. J., & Murray, C. (1994). *The bell curve: Intelligence and class structure in American life.* New York: Free Press.

Hollins, C. E. (1991). *It was fun from the beginning.* New York: Carlton Press.

Hunt, J. M. (1961). *Intelligence and experience.* New York: Ronald Press.

Jensen, A. R. (1969). How much can we boost IQ and scholastic achievement? *Harvard Educational Review, 33,* 1–123.

Lewis, O. (1961). *The children of Sanchez.* New York: Random House.

Lewis, R., Lovegrove, M. N., & Burman, E. (1991). Teachers' attitudes to classroom discipline. In Lovegrove, M. N., and Lewis, R. (Eds.), *Classroom Discipline.* Melbourne: Longman Cheshire.

McLaren, P. (1986) *Schooling as a ritual performance: Towards a political economy of educational symbols and gestures.* London: Routledge & Kegan Paul.

McLaren, P. (1995). *Critical pedagogy and predatory culture: Oppositional politics in a postmodern age.* New York: Routledge.

McLaren, P. (1997). *Revolutionary multiculturalism: Pedagogies of dissent for the new millennium.* Boulder, CO: Westview Press.

McLaren, P. (1998). *Life in Schools: An Introduction to Critical Pedagogy in the Foundations of Education.* White Plains, NY: Longman.

Meier, D. (1995). *The power of their ideas.* Boston: Beacon Press.

Miller, W. B. (1958). Lower class culture as a generating milieu of gang delinquency. *Journal of Social Issues, 14,* 5–19.

Morin, R. (1995, October 16–22). Across the racial divide: A new survey reveals the depths of our differences. *Washington Post Weekly Edition,* pp. 6–10.

Moynihan, D. P. (1965). *The Negro family: The case for national action.* Washington, DC: U.S. Department of Labor, U.S. Government Printing Office.

Oakes, J. (1984). *Keeping track: How schools structure inequality.* New Haven, CT: Yale University Press.

Oakes, J. (1992). *Educational matchmaking: Academic and vocational tracking in comprehensive high schools.* Santa Monica, CA: Rand.

Pearl, A. (1972). *The atrocity of education.* New York: Dutton.

Russell, B. (1927). Education. In *Selected papers* (87–110). New York: Random House–Modern Library.

Shaw, G. B. (1903). *Man and Superman.*

Tawney, R. H. (1964). *Equality.* London: Unwin Books. (First published in 1931.)

Trebach, A. S., & Ehlers, S. (1996, Summer). The war on our children. *The Drug Policy Letter, 30,* 13–17.

Valencia, R. R. (1997). *The evolution of deficit thinking in educational thought and practice.* New York: Falmer Press.

White, R. (1959). Motivation reconsidered: The concept of competence. *Psychological Review, LXVI,* 279–333.

Wigfield, A., Eccles, J. S., & Rodriguez, D. (1998). The Development of Children's Motivation in School Contexts. *Review of Research in Education, 23,* 73–118.

Willis, P. (with S. Jones, J. Canaan, & G. Hurd). (1990). *Common Culture: Symbolic work at play in the everyday cultures of the young.* Buckingham, London: Open University Press.

3

Democratic Practices as Manifested through Character Education

Paul F. Black, Slippery Rock University

In this chapter, the concept of democratic practices in education is enlarged to include the developments in the field of character education. The latter is a fundamental extension of the long and storied commitment of American society and culture to a common set of core values. Historically, inculcating values in the country's youth has been a function of the public school system, its teachers, administrators, and supportive parents. In the past, preservice teachers acquired knowledge of the value system from a wide variety of sources including the writings of historical figures, their own family customs, the beliefs of their religious affiliations, and the traditions of the society. Today preservice teachers and teacher educators can look directly to the field of character education for guidance in teaching values education. I begin by defining character education; I then describe the curricular forms it takes while I trace the interconnectedness of values and schooling from colonial times to the current developments in the decade of the 1990s. Character education comprises three elements:

1. A common core of shared or universal values
2. The belief that there are rational, objectively valid, universally accepted qualities to which people of all nations, creeds, races, socioeconomic statuses, and ethnicity subscribe
3. The belief that traits (qualities) transcend political persuasions as well as religious and ethnic differences

Thus, the first obligation of a school district when it addresses character education (establishes a program or makes a commitment) is to identify the universal values that will be the focus of the program and then make a commitment to teach those core values (Wiley, 1996). To assist school districts in identifying the core values, various organizations have developed, published, and disseminated curricular materials that delineate those values. For instance, the Heartwood Curriculum offers "seven character traits":

1. Courage
2. Loyalty
3. Justice
4. Respect
5. Hope
6. Honesty
7. Love

The Character Counts Coalition identifies six pillars:

1. Trustworthiness
2. Respect
3. Responsibility
4. Fairness
5. Caring
6. Citizenship

Some school districts values stipulate their own. For example, Baltimore identifies twenty-four core values, and St. Louis lists fifty characteristics. Dayton has a "word for the week" (Wiley, 1996). Others suggest the following concepts that define character education:

1. Honesty
2. Respect
3. Responsibility
4. Concern for the underdog
5. Friendship
6. Diligence

7. Prudence
8. Caring about
9. Self-esteem
10. Trust
11. Loyalty
12. Justice
13. Commitment
14. Self-discipline
15. Self-reliance (Woodfin, Sanchez, & Scalfini, 1996)

The number of characteristics identified in the preceding curricular models is less important than its conceptual framework. Historically, moral (character) education was a major part of the school experience. Ethical principles were extracted from the Bible, *Poor Richard's Almanac*, and the basic documents of our nation. Thomas Jefferson urged schools to stimulate students' minds and develop their reasoning faculties, cultivate their morals, and instill the precepts of virtue and order (Benson and Engeman, 1982). Thus, our founding fathers were convinced that ethical instruction was essential to maintaining the social system that they had created. Furthermore, the antecedents of character education began with those who knew that our nation rested on a profoundly moral idea. They were well aware that our democracy would rise or fall as a result of the citizenry's ability to respond to the moral challenge presented by this new form of government—challenges such as sitting in judgment of others in courtrooms, electing just judges and representatives, and enacting ethical laws (Ryan, 1996).

Specifically, Ben Franklin stated that "only a virtuous people are capable of freedom. . . . Nothing is of more importance for the public weal, than to form and train youth in wisdom and virtue" (Koch, 1965). Virtues identified in Franklin's *Autobiography* are:

1. Temperance
2. Silence
3. Order
4. Resolution
5. Frugality
6. Industry

7. Sincerity
8. Justice
9. Moderation
10. Cleanliness
11. Tranquility
12. Chastity
13. Humility

In the Northwest Ordinance of 1787 our forefathers provided that "religion, morality and knowledge [were] necessary to good government and happiness of mankind, schools and the means of education shall forever be encouraged" (deHuszar, Littlefield, & Littlefield, 1953). Thomas Jefferson extended this idea by placing his faith in the citizenry when he exclaimed, "I know of no safe repository for the ultimate powers of society but the people themselves, and if we think them not enlightened enough to exercise their control with a wholesome direction, the remedy is not to take it from them, but to increase their discretion by educators" (Jefferson, 1892–1899).

In the first half of the nineteenth century, three sources recognized the interrelationship between democratic practices and the need for moral and ethical conduct. These sources were McGuffey's Readers, de Tocqueville, and Horace Mann. McGuffey's Readers were widely employed in the public schools and include a number of historical examples of courage, honesty, gentleness, and other moral qualities. (Benson & Engeman, 1982). Alexis de Tocqueville wrote in his monumental two-volume treatise *Democracy in America* that America is great because she is good, remarking that if America ever ceases to be good it will then cease to be great (Ceasar, J., 1991). And finally the greatest educator of the nineteenth century, Horace Mann, believed that education should be universal, nonsectarian, and free, and that its aims should be social efficiency, civic virtue, and character rather than learning for the advancement of sectarian ends (Cubberley, 1947).

By the mid-nineteenth century (1863), John Swett, superintendent of public instruction in California, echoed the prevailing thought that moral training is an important part of public school education. This commitment to character education or the teaching of values continued into the twentieth century. As Robert Coles noted, "At Harvard, at least until 1902, it was the mission of the college to educate men of character and schools were for the education of the whole person and their responsibility extended to the inculcating of character" (Moral Life, 1990). Until World War I, ethics was a required course for undergraduates in most private liberal arts colleges of denominational background (Benson & Engeman, 1982). This perspective was reinforced by the legendary John Dewey when he wrote in his *Democracy and Education* that it is "commonplace in educational theory for the establishment of character to be the comprehensive aim of school instruction and disciplines." Two years later, in 1918, the National Education Association's (NEA) Commission on Secondary Education issued its Seven Cardinal Principles of Education, two of which were citizenship and ethical character. Even the Supreme Court in the landmark decision *Pierce v. Society of Sisters* (1923) involving the rights and responsibilities of parents and schools noted that public school teachers should be of good moral character and patriotic disposition [and] that certain studies plainly essential to good citizenship must be taught. Thus, citizenship and democratic practice became inexorably intertwined with ethics, morals, and education for character.

By the mid-twentieth century, the concept of a strong commitment by society to moral/ethical/character development in its schools seemed to be the rule rather than the exception. But the decades of the 1960s and 1970s eroded this perception with the popularization of the "value-free" curriculum. Teachers were taught at the university level that they should refrain from making judgments about student choices as "good" or "bad." Instead of teaching or inculcating values as to what was right or wrong they were encouraged to emphasize the process by which students made decisions. Students needed to clarify their value choices. Values became relative, and situational ethics prevailed. Proponents of character education found their core values being superseded by the values clarification movement. Educators such as Sidney Simon, Merrill Harmin, and Louis Raths led Americans, schools, and teacher educators astray with their values clarification and relativism, claimed the proponents of character education (Brooks & Goble, 1997).

Ironically some of the proponents of core values and character education who detested the values clarification movement included Lawrence Kohlberg. It was Kohlberg's Cognitive Moral Development Theory of the 1970s that swung the pendulum back to the character educators. Now traditional proponents of character education had a cognitive schema upon which to base their core universal values. Kohlberg became the bridge from the values clarification movement to the return of character development whose impetus is alive and well in the 1980s and 1990s.

With Kohlberg providing the intellectual framework, proponents turned to the states to set standards and mandate curricular policy including character education as we know it. Aided by the political climate that saw the presidency dominated for twelve years by former governors, the proponents found allies in the state legislatures. The distrust of Washington DC and the political conservatism of the times contributed to the successful efforts. Reminding state legislators of their responsibility for education under the Tenth Amendment, character education proponents prevailed. Specifically, New Hampshire and Washington State led the way by incorporating character education in their standards for teacher certification. Washington requires a study of values in public schools. New Hampshire requires "character and citizenship" at both pre- and in-service levels. (In its requirements for certificate renewal New Hampshire mandates sixty clock hours of staff development every three years—five hours of which must address character and citizenship.) The following is a summary of state-level activity regarding character education (this list is not intended to be comprehensive):

1. California requires it.
2. Maine, North Carolina, Oregon, Tennessee, Hawaii, New Mexico, and Washington have laws requiring schools to teach moral or ethics education.
3. Virginia and Louisiana have social studies standards in character and citizenship.
4. West Virginia integrates it into the content curriculum.
5. Vermont includes it in the Common Core of Learning.
6. New Hampshire does not require it in curriculum but requires each school board to develop a policy stating how character education is being taught.
7. Iowa passed a law encouraging but not mandating it.
8. Ohio provides a research guide. (South Carolina is writing one.)
9. Kentucky wrote a nonmandated curriculum.
10. Alabama mandates a minimum of ten minutes of instruction each day.

11. Alaska, Kansas, Minnesota, Pennsylvania, and Texas have no state-level activity. (Wiley, 1996; Brooks & Goble, 1997)

Because of the democratic nature of our public schools, state legislators are not the only source of character education initiatives. Other sources are local boards of education (school boards), school administrators, advisory groups, parent-teacher associations, and business-related organizations. This format has produced a system that is responsive "to the people" at the local level (Brooks & Goble, 1997).

Specifically a number of communities across the nation have developed a community-based approach to character education. School districts in towns and cities such as Milton, Vermont; Santa Ynez, California; Duncanville and Tyler, Texas; and Woodland Hills, Bethel Park, and Mt. Lebanon, Pennsylvania, have involved the business sector, law enforcement, community-based organizations, and the faith establishment in reaching agreement on common core values that can be taught and reinforced (Brooks & Goble, 1997).

The awareness that homes and schools must return to the teaching of core values has enjoyed a startling increase since 1990. This awareness was capped when the U.S. House of Representatives passed Joint Resolution 366, which calls for a week in October to be designated as National Character Counts Week. This event began in 1994 and has continued to this day (Brooks & Goble, 1997). Complementing this was the publication of *Finding Common Ground* in 1994 by the Freedom Forum First Amendment Center at Vanderbilt University, which highlighted character education and resources available to schools. The national YMCA also established a series of character development activities for its members. All this activity was in addition to the long-range curricular impact of school-based organizations such as Heartwood, Character Education Partnership, Jefferson Center for Character Education, and so on, discussed earlier. (A comprehensive list of organizations and their educational contributions/resources is available in Rusnak's *An Integrated Approach to Character Education*.)

In his 1997 State of the Union Address, President Clinton somewhat ironically stated that "today the enduring worth of our nation lies in our values and our soaring spirit." Furthermore, this decade has witnessed the institutionalization of the service-learning component in our basic and higher education curricula. Many schools and districts have even made it a graduation requirement. It may well be that the 1990s will be remembered as the decade when the teaching of citizenship was restored to homes and schools.

In the previous historical review of the commitment of our country to democratic practices as reflected through character education developments, it can be seen that American education at all levels has carried a clear moral mandate that has been expressed in the instructions for citizenship in the primary grades or the more sophisticated moral philosophy of higher education. Historically, public education in America has been justified by the need in a democratic society for literate, informed, and moral citizens. Thus, it has fallen to the schools to assume leadership in reaffirming the role of character education (Character Education Task Force, 1982).

REFERENCES

Benson, C. S., & Engeman, T. S. (1982). *Amoral America*. Durham, NC: Carolina Academic Press.

Brooks, B., & Goble, F. (1997). *The case for character education: The role of the school in teaching values and virtue.* Northridge, CA: Studio 4 Productions.

Ceasar, J. W. Political science, political culture, and the role of the intellectual. In K. Masugi, Ed., *Interpreting Tocqueville's Democracy in America.* Savage, MD: Rowman & Littlefield.

Character Education Task Force (1982, August). *A reawakening: Character education and the role of the school board member*, pp. 2–3.

Cubberley, E. (1947). *Public education in the United States.* Boston: Houghton Mifflin.

Dewey, J. (1966). *Democracy and education.* New York: Free Press.

deHuszar, G., Littlefield, H., & Littlefield, A. (Eds.). (1953). *Basic American documents.* Ames, IA: Littlefield, Adams.

Haynes, C. C., Thomas, O., & Fernuson, T. (1994). *Finding common ground: A guide to religious liberty in public schools.* Nashville, TN: The First Ammendment Center.

Koch, A. (Ed.). (1965). *The American enlightenment.* New York: George Braziller.

The moral life of American schoolchildren: Special report. (1990, March). *Teacher Magazine*, 41.

Rusnak, T. (Ed.). (1998). *An integrated approach to character education.* Thousand Oaks, CA: Corwin Press.

Ryan, K. (1996, Spring). Staff development's golden opportunity in character education. *Journal of Staff Development, 17*(2), 6–9.

Wiley, L. (1996, Spring). The role of staff development in implementing character development. *Journal of Staff Development, 17*(2), 50–52.

Woodfin, D., Sanchez, K., & Scalfini, S. (1996, Spring). Community involvement jumpstarts a district-wide character education program. *Journal of Staff Development, 17*(2), 24–27.

The Writings of Thomas Jefferson (1892–99). New York: Putnam.

4

Democracy, Schools, and Cultural Minority Groups

Armando Laguardia, Washington State University, Vancouver

One of the challenges to modern industrialized democracies has been to make available to *all* its young citizens an education that prepares them for social inclusion and democratic citizenship. Inclusion, participation, and equality are integral parts of the seven critical dimensions or attributes that apply to democratic educational practices proposed in this book (Laguardia and Pearl, chapter 2 of this book).

This chapter offers an analysis of the historical response of modern democracies to this challenge and a vision for the future by arguing that the sociopolitical environment has been and continues to be of tremendous importance in the attempts to incorporate cultural minority groups in schools in the industrialized democracies, including those of the United States. Moreover, this chapter examines how key democratic institutions have helped move this nation toward the goal of providing equal educational opportunities.

Recognizing the role that politics has played in realigning priorities in American education, this analysis examines the impact that recent political agendas have had on our new school reform movement and argues that innovative political actions are necessary to increase the ability of our schools to serve as institutions that promote democracy in general while addressing the increasing demands for equal educational opportunities.

Finally, this chapter discusses implications for public school teachers and teacher education, including the need to define and participate in policy formation, prepare the teaching force for a multicultural democracy, and address the imperative to diversify the teaching profession in the United States.

AN INTERNATIONAL PERSPECTIVE

Ethnic and cultural groups have become integral to industrialized nations, in part for economic reasons. Industrialized nations have, over time, adopted and modified immigration policies to make them consistent with their need for a source of cheaper labor. Immigrants are typically accepted into host countries to satisfy unskilled labor demands, although host countries have more recently shifted their demand for labor sources with higher educational levels and skills in technological occupations. Immigrants, however, remain an important source of unskilled labor in such sectors as agriculture, service, and manufacturing and tend to concentrate in those low-paying occupations that are generally neither sought nor desired by native populations.

In addition to immigration practices, some nations have achieved an increase in racially and ethnically diverse populations through colonization and expansionist policies. The result has been inclusion, though not necessarily integration, of new racial, linguistic, and ethnic communities.

Where it does occur, the integration of immigrants into mainstream culture has often advanced slowly and at considerable human cost, resulting in clashes between the youngest members of these immigrant groups and the institutions, particularly the schools, with which they come into contact with in their newly adopted environment.

Attempts to integrate disparate cultural groups into societies and institutions have been met with obstacles, some of them complex and deep seated. Racial, religious, and ethnic intolerance abound in the third world, and the schism observed between the educational opportunities of the elite classes in those countries and those of the lower social strata, including immigrants, is deeper than in many industrial democracies.

Unlike third-world countries, democratic states are by definition committed in theory to promoting equality for all its citizens. For this reason, the integration of cultural minority groups in democratic nations presents a unique conflict: their democratic nature requires them to provide equal opportunities to all their citizens, or as Barber (1998) puts it, "The challenge in a democracy is to maintain excellence while extending educational opportunity to everyone" (p. 223).

It has been noted by others (Sigel & Hoskin, 1991) that democracies struggle with educating cultural, racial, and ethnic groups they desire to bring into the mainstream of their societies. In their book, *Education for Democratic Citizenship: A Challenge for Multiethnic Societies*, Sigel and Hoskins analyze the common experiences and challenges of industrialized democracies, including Great Britain, France, Japan, Israel, the United States, and the Netherlands. They arrive at several important conclusions. First, the governments of these countries, they opine, are constrained by their pasts. Colonial stereotypes persist, such as those that confer to colonized people inferior status and view them as a danger to mainstream society and the *status quo* (p. 210).

Secondly, despite their monopoly on legitimate political authority, these governments have not utilized their mandate to take on the thorny issues presented by their immigrant populations. Sigel and Hoskin opine that in these democracies political debate has rarely challenged existing policy assumptions; policy, therefore, is almost universally incremental, reactive, and explained in ad hoc terms. Education in these democracies remains, to a large extent, the domain of the privileged and the established middle classes and is not extended to all other groups in a fashion that is truly democratic.

Mitchell and Salisbury (1996) surveyed forty-two of the world's nations regarding their attempts to educate cultural minority groups. The countries studied fell primarily into two groups: "cultural pluralists" and "assimilationists." Countries identified as cultural pluralists (i.e., Australia, Colombia, Guinea, India, Israel, Japan, Liberia, the Netherlands, Norway, Paraguay, Singapore, Spain, Sri Lanka, and the United States) adhere to the general theory that the strength of a nation rests in the diversity of its people. On the other hand, assimilationist countries (i.e., Bahrain, Canada, the People's Republic of China, Congo, Austria, El Salvador, Guyana, Kenya, Taiwan, and Thailand) encourage the microcultures within their borders to reject their cultural heritage in favor of adopting or assimilating the value system of the dominant culture.

The forty-two countries responded to questions about administration, teacher certification, languages of instruction, school integration, the teaching of the history of indigenous people, and the screening of instructional materials. The researchers concluded that far too few countries have seriously addressed national problems of racism, sexism, stereotyping, and ethnocentrism in their schools.

The findings are reflected in the U.S. schools of the early twenty-first century. All these democratic nations are faced with the dual challenge of extending educational opportunities and preparing for democratic citizenship increasing numbers of young nonwhite minority citizens. Here, a school achievement gap between ethnic minority students and members of the majority white population is recognized as one of the major challenges of schools and teachers. Preparation for democratic citizenship is crucial in determining whether these groups will either become part of the mainstream or remain behind, unable to contribute to this increasingly technological credential-requiring society.

THE NATIONAL CONTEXT

The education of ethnic, racial, and cultural groups in the United States has followed some of the same patterns identified by Sigel and Hoskins (1991) and Mitchell and Salisbury (1996) in other democracies.

Cultural, racial, and ethnic minorities (including European immigrants, African-Americans, Asian-Americans, and Hispanics) have been accepted into the United States when needed to fulfill the labor demands of the U.S. economy or as a result of migration to seek political freedom and economic opportunities.

The largest racial and ethnic groups—Native Americans, Mexican-Americans, and African-Americans—were notable exceptions to the typical pattern of integration. The first two groups (Native Americans and Mexican-Americans) became citizens through expansionist policies initiated in the last century. Native Americans were systematically segregated in reservations created by the federal government and educated in Indian schools operated by the Bureau of Indian Affairs for the purpose of acculturation. Mexican-American children were excluded from public schools and educated in segregated schools. African-Americans were brought as slave labor and systematically denied education during and after enslavement and remain largely segregated in inferior schools despite constitutionally mandated desegregation.

For these ethnic/cultural groups, integration into our schools has been difficult at best, and the reality has been a persistent disparity in educational outcomes. This was true as well for European ethnic groups (Jews, Italians, Irish) who experienced and combated wholesale discrimination in American public schools in the latter nineteenth century and the early part of this century (Tyack & Hansot, 1982).

Attempts to redress educational inequities experienced by the largest ethnic and racial groups of color (African-Americans, Hispanics, Asian-Americans, and Native Americans) are increasingly important because of the heightened value placed on educational attainment in a literate, technological, and credential-demanding society.

Our "common" schools were created as public institutions with the ideal of preparing their participants for democratic citizenship. They were visualized by Thomas Jefferson to develop that "natural aristocracy" of the few whose talents justly deserved to be developed for the benefit of society. Horace Mann and the common school advocates succeeded in expanding the notion of public schools to universal education. For these reformers education was to be "the balance wheel" of society (Kirst, 1984). The common public schools have come to epitomize a stable egalitarian mechanism designed to moderate pernicious social inequalities.

Under these expectations the United States has attempted to expand educational opportunities to increasing numbers of its population. Currently, the United States enrolls a higher percentage of young people in secondary school and college than any other Western nation. Our system has grown steadily more egalitarian. As recently as 1940, fewer than 50 percent of the pupils in this country completed high school; by 1984, 75 percent were graduates. In 1974 the United States had the highest secondary school and college enrollments in the developed world, with 82 percent of fifteen-to-eighteen-year-olds enrolled in school and 52 percent of twenty-to-twenty-four-year-olds enrolled in postsecondary education.

DEMOCRATIC INSTITUTIONS AND EQUAL EDUCATION IN THE UNITED STATES

The struggle of cultural minority groups to avail themselves of an education has been aided by the full range of government (judicial, executive, and legislative). Democratic traditions and democratic remedies have been and might continue to be the key to change in America's schools for these groups. The courts have been particularly instrumental in mandating equality of educational opportunity, beginning with the landmark 1954 U.S. Supreme Court school desegregation decision in *Brown v. Board of Education*, which was critical in ushering in the Civil Rights Movement of the 1960s.

Segregationist American educational policies aimed at African-American and other students of color were outlawed by the U.S. Supreme Court in *Brown v. Board of Education*. Legal recourse has since been used by a variety of other ethnic and cultural groups to achieve expanded educational rights.

Another Supreme Court decision, *Lau v. Nichols,* established the rights of students to an education regardless of their linguistic background. Title IX of the Higher Education Amendments and Public Law 94-142 were legislative avenues for the equal access of disabled and female students to school services.

Executive orders by Presidents Kennedy and Johnson threatened to withhold public funds to pressure public and private institutions to take decisive steps to counteract previous discrimination and to expand employment and educational opportunities to minority, female, and disabled students in K–12 and postsecondary education. The result has been a plethora of lawsuits, congressional legislation, and social and educational programs on behalf of groups who have traditionally been denied equal opportunity within the U.S. educational system.

The link between equality per se and equality of educational opportunity grew steadily in importance to become the foremost mission of U.S. educational policy throughout much of the second half of this century (Howe, 1997).

THE STRUGGLE FOR THE NEW DIRECTION OF AMERICAN PUBLIC SCHOOLS

Beginning in 1980 political events, including the election of Ronald Reagan as president, brought about a sharp shift in focus from equality of education, integration, and cultural pluralism to school "choice," the privatization of public schools, and the mandate for accountability, academic standards, and testing. The report of the National Commission on Excellence in Education, *A Nation at Risk: The Imperative for Educational Reform* (1983), gave us a wide-ranging critique of public education and advocated choice and higher standards at the expense of the impulse toward egalitarianism in our schools.

A Nation at Risk captured the interest of state legislators and governors who eagerly examined the remedies proposed by that report and launched an extraordinary number of blue-ribbon commissions and panels to study the current state of education and propose actions for the emerging new goals of educational reform. The composition of state legislatures and state governorships became more politically conservative and reactive to the findings of the report blaming U.S. schools for a perceived lack of economic competitiveness. State legislatures were flooded with bills patterned after the report's recommendations to raise educational standards and stem what *A Nation at Risk* referred to as "the rising tide of mediocrity."

Venturing beyond the usual proposals for educational change, *A Nation at Risk* called for increased required credits in the academic core and more testing for a wider range of purposes, including grade-to-grade promotion and graduation from high school. The report also urged longer school days and a longer academic year, higher teacher salaries accompanied by tougher certification and entry requirements, an upgrade of the technology of schooling, and close state monitoring of school performance. These strategies were adopted by many states and were given expression in the form of mandates for "accountability."

The new reform movement approaches the task of restructuring schools quite differently than reforms of the past. Although it pushed for the decentralization of decision-making power, in reality the new reform efforts are characterized by centralized, state-mandated standards and tests, allowing powerful state officials and legislators to steer schools from afar and shifting the balance of power from the local to the state levels, and thereby undermining the expressed, if not actual, commitment to decentralization.

Advocates for minority students are wary about the impact the current reform initiatives might have. They believe that the public schools have been maligned by a "manufactured crisis" (Berliner & Biddle, 1995). According to tests used to gauge student achievement, though our schools meet the needs of the middle and affluent students, the real problem lies with the poor and marginalized minorities and the inability on the part of schools to educate them adequately. The direction laid out by the reform agenda is viewed as a threat to our democratic schools and to the educational opportunities afforded cultural minorities and other marginalized youth (Goodlad, 1997; Apple & Beane, 1995; Meier, 1995; Lasch, 1995; Levine, 1996; Ochoa & Espinoza, 1996).

The National Coalition of Advocates for Students (NCAS, 1992), a nation-wide network of twenty-two child advocacy organizations working to improve educational opportunity for the most vulnerable students, sounded the alarm about school reform in an article appearing in *Education Week* entitled "'World Class' Standards Are a Cruel Hoax Without a New Bill of Rights for U.S. School Children." The NCAS opposed proposals by the National Council on Educational Standards and Testing to enforce national education standards and nationwide testing in five core subjects.

The NCAS called for a national dialogue on attaining educational standards and issued a "bill of rights" for U.S. children emphasizing the accommodation of diverse abilities and needs, as well as respect for native languages and culture.

The NCAS questioned whether top-down school reforms, such as heightened standards and more testing, would truly address the nation's concerns over U.S. competitiveness in a global economy. The Coalition pointed to the competitive edge attributed to Germany and Japan as owing more to the extensive social support system for children in those countries than the quality of education in their schools.

More recently, other educators (Apple, 1996; Berliner & Biddle, 1995; Kozol, 1991; Spring, 1997) have criticized the current reform agenda on the basis of what they consider to be its faulty premises, namely, (1) public schooling has failed us and should be made more competitive through privatization; (2) inadequate schooling is responsible for the lack of "competitiveness" of American workers; (3) more good-paying jobs await us if we prepare appropriately for a postmodern "global economy."

Berliner and Biddle (1995), in particular, reject what they view as the myths promulgated by public education critics and used to promote the reshaping of public education. They contend that, contrary to the drop in SAT scores cited by critics of public education, among certain groups these are actually rising. They point to the increase in the rate of minority high school graduates and this group's college enrollment as evidence that not all is broken in American schools. They also claim that statistics that purport to show a rise in illiteracy are skewed because schools are now educating the traditionally disenfranchised in ever larger numbers (Kirst, 1984). Deborah Meier (1995) exemplifies the arguments in the following quote from her book *The Power of Their Ideas: Lessons for America from a Small School in Harlem:*

> Schools are not the cause of any competitive disadvantage the United States may or may not face. American productivity remains high and American workers relatively well educated. They work longer and harder than workers in other industrial nations, and with less job security. There are, furthermore, plenty of "over-educated" amongst the unemployed. We needn't be ashamed of our country or our schools. The reason to reform our schools is that we believe in fairness and democracy. We can no longer defend the discrepancies between the haves and have-nots, nor pay the price for the social unrest these discrepancies create. Ultimately if we stick together we can do far better for everyone. (p. 80)

The mission of the new reform movement is also considered too narrowly focused on the relationship between schools and economic objectives. Educators are alarmed that the new reformers diminish the importance of public schools as the vehicles for the creation of a democratic citizenry. In explaining the forces that united teachers to form the Institute for Democracy in Education, George Wood (1995) explains that

> The concern that pulled these teachers together was what the reform movement was saying about the purpose of public education. Virtually every reform proposal was laced with language that made it clear that the main reason to be concerned about public education was economic. But nothing was said about the democratic or public mission of schools. The issue here was that if the main reason for school reform is just to prepare workers, then the civic, democratic mission would be overlooked. (p. 12)

THE NEW POLITICS IN EDUCATION

The impact that conservatives have had on recent American politics, and consequently on educational policy, cannot be ignored. Conservatives have formed a voting coalition that elected two presidents and shifted the balance of power in the U.S. Congress, state legislatures, governors' offices, and local school boards.

The emerging strength of Christian conservatives, in particular, is one of the most important historic developments of our time. The rise of Christian conservatives to a position of respectability is detailed by Ralph Reed in his 1996 book *Active Faith: How Christians Are Changing the Soul of American Politics.*

The Christian Coalition has acted as a powerful ally of the Republican Party, and it came as no surprise that the Republican platform of 1996 reflected the influence of the Coalition in its opposition to birth control education in the schools, but its support for teaching abstinence; its opposition to multiculturalism, but its advocacy for patriotic and Western civilization–related curriculum coupled with a pledge to make English the official language in the United States; and its campaign to abolish the Department of Education, thus diminishing public school support, and instead advocating school vouchers and school choice.

The "Contract with America" political agenda supported some of the same goals, including school choice and local efforts to privatize schools.

Think tanks such as the Heritage Foundation, the Cato Institute, the Hudson Institute, and others have also played an influential role in the advancement of the conservative agenda. Beginning with the John Olin Foundation, conservative think tanks began to organize a cadre of intellectuals to openly support freedom and capitalism, because in their view colleges and universities were hopelessly controlled by left-wing intellectuals (Spring, 1997).

Armed with large budgets and public relations staffs, these conservative institutes actively promoted the reform of public education. They operated on the notion that it is as important to develop ideas as it is to disseminate them. Spring (1997, p. 27) details their plan to implement an anti–public school agenda via the following methods: (1) creating foundations and institutes that fund research and policy statements supportive of school choice, privatization of public schools, and, more recently, charter schools; (2) identifying scholars to do research, write policy statements, and lecture at public forums that are favorable to school choice, privatization of public schools, and charter schools; (3) financing conferences to bring like-minded scholars together for the sharing of ideas and the creation of edited books; and (4) paying scholars to write newspaper opinion pieces that are then distributed to hundreds of newspapers across the country.

The plan has led to a coherent agenda implemented by state legislatures, school boards, and the U.S. Congress, thereby creating new policies, standards, and assessments that together are dramatically reshaping American schools. Standards and tests have dominated attention in the early phase of our new school reform movement. Although standardized testing is seldom used in day-to-day work, the testing mentality has permeated public education. Teachers are dedicating more classroom time to preparing students for state tests because standardized test scores are used to measure the efficacy of their schools. Those schools that fail to improve test scores are singled out, and in some cases become candidates for "reconstitution," a euphemism for dramatic structural reorganization and mass teacher dismissals to make way for the selection of a fresh teacher workforce geared toward implementing the new achievement goals. Not surprisingly, many of these "reconstituted" schools are in communities with high percentages of low-income and minority families.

The new assessments are confirming what previous standardized tests revealed—namely, that school performance as reflected in standardized tests is highly correlated with the socioeconomic status of the students tested. Students from well-rooted communities and educated middle-income families consistently perform at higher levels in standardized tests than those from poor communities and uneducated families.

School superintendents and school board members have voiced some of the same reservations about testing heard from classroom teachers. One urban school superintendent in the state of Washington expressed his concerns on the record about the impact of high-stakes testing on the poor and minority students in his school district (Parsley, 1997). He noted that a careful analysis of recent statewide assessments showed that the information generated by the latest state assessment was identical to data already evident in other standardized test results. Parsley observed that youngsters who come from poverty who are subject to frequent moves, or who have limited proficiency in English, perform poorly on achievement measures. Like many other educators across the country, Parsley asks the obvious question:

> What accommodations will be made for special needs students, and what resources will be provided to assist students in meeting the new requirements? Without additional support for education, high standards may cause marginal learning gains, but not the breakthrough results desired by policy makers. (p. 32)

While a number of factors contribute to the poor quality of education available to ethnic/racial minority groups, one of the most important has been the historical inequity in funding for predominantly minority schools when compared to the schools of white middle-class Americans.

Howe (1997) observes that, though the ideal of equal educational opportunities grew in importance, so much so that promoting educational opportunity was the foremost mission in U.S. educational policy throughout much of the second half of this century, in terms of school funding, the drive for equality has come up short. Expenditure disparities currently range between $2,000 and $20,000 per pupil. Contrary to that much-overused slogan that "you can't solve problems by throwing money at them," the effects of inadequate funding on educational quality and therefore equality are all too apparent.

Schools with a high student population of Mexican-Americans, for example, were not funded at the same level as predominantly Anglo schools. In Texas, schools with large Mexican-descent student bodies received about three-fifths the appropriations destined for Anglo schools as recently as the 1970s (Acuna, 1988). In Bexar County in Texas, a poor "Chicano district" with five times less property tax than more affluent districts, schools received less state aid per pupil than those in the wealthier neighboring Anglo district. The imbalance was caused by the disparity in the wealth of the districts' tax bases.

Affected Chicanos took their case to court to demand funding equity. In *Serrano v. Priest,* initiated in 1968, Serrano sued the California state treasurer on the grounds that his son was receiving an inferior education based on the fact that local property taxes financed the schools. In 1971 the California Supreme Court held that financing primarily through local property taxes failed to provide equal protection under the law. In short, money determined the quality of education. Therefore if equal educational opportunity was a right, the rich and the poor school districts had to be funded equally. The U.S. Supreme Court (1976) upheld the California Supreme Court ruling in *Serrano* but limited its decision to California, holding that the financing system violated the state constitution's equal protection clause by denying equal access to education.

In another landmark decision in 1968, *San Antonio School District v. Rodriguez,* the Supreme Court found that the U.S. Constitution did not include equal education as a fundamental right. Justice Thurgood Marshall summed up the importance of the ruling at the time: "The majority's holding can only be seen as a retreat from historic commitment to equality of educational opportunity and insupportable acquiescence in a system which deprives children in their earliest years of the chance to reach their full potential as citizens." (Bambritta, Milne, & Davis, 1991, p. 151.)

The discrepancies in funding in different school districts, as well as within the same school district, persist in the United States, with cultural minority and poor students disproportionately attending the schools and districts with less financial support.

The tracking of minority students within schools is another significant factor contributing to the inequality of educational achievement. Tracking has been in use since the 1920s. Our tracked curriculum, with its "ability-grouped" academic classes, has been hailed by some as functional, scientific, and democratic. Initially, tracking appeared to be an educationally sound approach for providing all students an education appropriate to their abilities. Because of its widespread use and acceptance in official and unofficial forms, tracking has limited the educational opportunities of large numbers of minority students who are disproportionately placed in lower tracks or less demanding courses. One longtime student of tracking and its impact on minority students (Oakes, 1996) asserts that

> Considerable research demonstrates that students do not profit from enrollment in low track classes; they do not learn as much as comparably skilled students in heterogeneous classes; they have less access than other students to knowledge, engaging learning activities, and resources. Thus school tracking practices create racially separate programs that provide minority children with restricted educational opportunities and outcomes. (p. 82)

In her analysis of tracking in two school districts, Oakes (1996) came to disturbing conclusions about tracking and school curriculum segregation. The tracking systems were found to be pervasive and harmful to African-American and Latino students in three ways: (1) disproportionate assignment to low-track classes and exclusion from accelerated classes, resulting in de facto segregation; (2) inferior opportunities to learn; and (3) lower achievement.

Oakes and Stuart-Wells (1998), in subsequent research, found that even when schools attempt to change tracking practices, they are challenged by formidable cultural and political obstacles, including deeply held beliefs about intelligence, racial differences, social stratification, and privilege.

In their research, Oakes and Stuart-Wells found that teachers who offered advanced courses to all students instead of a select few were severely criticized by the parents of identified gifted students. What upset the parents most was not the quality of courses offered, but rather that their children's privileged curriculum would be compromised if opened to all students.

THE ATTACK ON MULTICULTURALISM IN THE SCHOOLS

The notion of a multicultural educational system has won the support of professional educational organizations, including the National Education Association, the American Association of Colleges of Teacher Educators, the Association of Teacher Educators, the Council of Chief State School Officers, the National Council for Social Studies, and many other state and regional organizations that have expressed tacit support for cultural diversity in countless proclamations, curriculum guidelines, and policy statements.

But the call for an inclusive multicultural education has drawn fire from conservative theorists, politicians, and commentators (Webster, 1997; Ravitch & Finn, 1987; Hirsh, 1996). Criticism of multicultural education is frequently based on a limited perception of its purposes. Critics tend to view it only as curricular change, overlooking the impact of the political and legal antecedents previously mentioned and the real past and present discrimination that must be addressed. Multiculturalists repeatedly advocate an education that embraces and represents all our citizens (Banks, 1997; Nieto, 1996; Grant & Sleeter, 1994), but they are portrayed as dangerous separatists by their critics. Organized political opposition by the religious right, the Republican Party, and conservative state legislators is challenging the inclusion of cultural pluralism in the new curricular standards. The addition of multicultural perspectives in the new state social studies curricula has prompted heated discussions and delays in the issuance of state guidelines. Conservatives argue that it is time to stop focusing on racial differences and to eliminate programs that are specifically designed to benefit cultural minorities.

This mentality has seriously affected programs and services for minority students. College admission programs benefiting minorities, for instance, have been eroded by the attack on affirmative action strategies, as have programs for second-language minority students in the K–12 school systems.

The discussions about the education of cultural minority groups in the United States has recently centered on curriculum content and adaptation rather than on issues of equality and access. In fact, much of the attack on multiculturalism (i.e., the conflict about the Portland, Oregon, African-American baseline essays) is leveled at questions of historical accuracy and the proper balance that Western and European perspectives are given in the accounting of world and American history.

I would argue that while those issues are important, they are only part of the multicultural education terrain. National political agendas are driving educational practices these days more than at any other period. The impact of the new school reform movement is testimony to the influence that political pressures can have on school curriculum, testing, classroom practices, and student services.

One of our concerns in a democracy should be whether those reforms promote the inclusive goals of our democratic educational systems and provide an avenue toward equality for cultural minority students. According to the National Center for Education Statistics (2004) whites continue to outperform minority groups in reading, writing, and mathematics. The number of books in the home was associated with higher achievement, as was parents' education. The level of poverty in the school as measured by the percentage of students eligible for free and reduced lunch was negatively associated with student achievement in 2003 (National Center for Education Statistics, 2004).

Curiously, some of the necessary ingredients for significant improvement of schools are conspicuously missing from the reform agenda. Absent are comprehensive plans to improve teacher effectiveness through preservice and in-service teacher preparation, an essential component of successful reform (Darling-Hammond & McLaughlin, 1995), the reduction of class sizes together with the increase of much-needed planning time for teachers, and improved instructional resources.

The inferior and therefore unequal allocation of educational resources to poorer communities is one of the most important roadblocks to higher academic achievement by minorities. The United States, unlike other industrialized democracies, operates an educational system that allows for great inequalities in per student expenditures for schools. That inequality of expenditures leads frequently to enhanced opportunities for the children of the affluent. The concern about the disparate funding of American schools prompted Spring (1997) to comment:

> It is reprehensible that the Republican and Democratic parties remain silent on the issues of unequal funding of schools. Without equal funding of schools, academic standards and high stakes tests will widen the gap

between the rich and the poor. The efforts of the New Democrats to make credentials and test scores a key feature of the labor market will, without equal school funding, sharpen social class lines. The United States will become a mandarin society with tight controls over the ideas to which students are exposed in school. The poor will be taught to love the very system of academic standards and tests that condemns them to a life of low-paying and meaningless work. (p. 118)

Equalizing educational opportunity through privatization with vouchers has been the solution to the problem of minority underperformance advocated by conservative reformers. But the evidence does not support that contention. Drawing on empirical research on choice, two renowned students of educational reform, Fuller and Elmore (1996), conclude that increasing educational choice with vouchers is likely to increase separation of students by race, social class, and cultural background, and that greater choice in public education is unlikely, by itself, to increase either the variety of programs available to students or the overall performance of schools. According to Fuller and Elmore, only when coupled with strong educational improvement measures will choice improve variety and performance.

Witte's (1996) study of the Milwaukee public schools voucher program offered to poor parents who choose private schools suggests that achievement results are weak and variable and favor neither public nor private schools. However, school choice serves the interests of parents who want to send their children to religious or private schools.

Whitty, Power, and Halpin (1998) examined recent reform efforts in England and Wales, the United States, Australia, New Zealand, and Sweden. They reviewed the research evidence on the impact of reform to date in those countries. They conclude that, at the same time they appear to devolve power to individual schools and parents, these governments have actually been increasing their own capacity to "steer" the systems at a distance. They also conclude that there is no strong evidence to support the educational benefits claimed by the proponents of the reforms; on the contrary, they say there is considerable evidence that these reforms are enabling already advantaged schools and parents to maximize their favorable position.

Hatcher (1996) argues that, if these damaging equity effects are to be avoided, there is an urgent need to redress the balance between consumer rights and citizen rights in education. They recognize that opening schools to local democratic political action will attract reactionary and progressive forces. But whatever the risks, the researchers remind us that this opening is precisely where a "democratic politics of education starts" (p. 142), and that the outcomes are not inevitably unfavorable.

One of the complications, they point out, is the inability of progressive educators and citizens to develop a concept of public education that looks significantly different from the education they have spent time critiquing. New directions will require "a revitalization of civil society and the development of new forms of democracy more suited to contemporary societies. We now need to experiment with and evaluate new forms of association in the public sphere within which citizens rights in education policy—and indeed other areas of public policy—can be reasserted against current trends toward both a restricted and authoritarian version of the state and marketized civil society" (Whitty, Power, & Halpin, 1998, p. 134).

IMPLICATIONS FOR TEACHER PREPARATION

Given these conditions, where should efforts to regain the lost momentum toward educational opportunity for cultural minority groups begin? It must begin—with the recognition of the importance of political participation by education professionals, including teacher educators—with the redirection of public education toward the mission of preparing all students to be what I call "cultural democratic citizens" who understand culture in all its manifestations and its influence on our society. The preparation of students in this area is not to be viewed as a subversive activity but as a responsibility reflected in our school missions and educational standards.

This chapter underscores the continued importance of politics and policy formation in efforts to reshape schools. Our schools are politically charged institutions governed through citizen and policy maker participation. Therefore the conditions of cultural minority students will not be significantly affected without political actions, policy redirections, and programmatic decisions that produce results. These actions will require the participation of educators in the politic/policy arena in order to guarantee that schools and colleges provide the equal *access* and *participation* required by democratic institutions.

Since 1980 new political and ideological priorities for school reform have all but halted the slow progress toward educational equity for cultural minorities that is considered essential to a working democracy.

Education for cultural minority groups has suffered in part from the lack of a clear, cogent definition of objectives that can be supported and promoted within the political arena. It is imperative that we redefine education in America today, taking into account the democratic tradition. We must articulate how our educational system views the relationship between culture and education. This is particularly important given the sensitivity surrounding this issue and the pervasiveness of misinformation about what constitutes an education for cultural democracy.

The following definition may serve this purpose: an education for cultural democracy teaches about the nature of human cultures and their characteristics; exposes students to the participation and conflicts of the many cultural groups in our nation's history and development; addresses the educational needs of all our students regardless of their race, language, or culture; prepares students to be productive members of their communities, state, and nation, and prepares them to exercise their rights in a democratic society.

The task of changing the political priorities for education is daunting. A series of significant actions must be taken jointly. The changes will require sustained political organization and compromise. New priorities for education must be debated and included in the national and state political party platforms. The unfairness of present school funding and the disparate use of resources within schools to the disadvantage of marginalized students must be changed. Many educators are becoming active participants in this process. Not only are they taking organizational positions on important policy issues, such as school vouchers, testing, and school access for cultural minority groups, they are also playing an increasingly important role in informing the policy debate in these areas from their unique perspective as professionals in the nation's schools and colleges.

Teacher educators have special responsibilities in two areas: (1) the preparation of teachers for our multicultural democratic society and (2) the provision of equitable access to the teaching profession by members of underrepresented cultural groups.

John Dewey, the preeminent American Education philosopher, expressed concerns about the obstacles to achieving a democratic education. According to Dewey the principle obstacle to achieving democratic education was the powerful alliance of class privilege with philosophies of education. Dewey's concern was with the ideas implied by the democratic society and the application of these ideas to education. "The price that democratic societies will have to pay for their continuing health," Dewey argued, "is the elimination of an oligarchy—the most exclusive and dangerous of all—that attempts to monopolize the benefits of intelligence and the best methods for the profit of a few privileged ones" (Dewey, 1913, p. 127). Dewey was obviously in support of an *all*-inclusive education. He expressed the notion that the best way to achieve democracy is to initiate children into a form of social life characteristic of democracy: a community of full participation and "conjunct communicated experience" as preparation for living in a democracy (Ross, 1998).

In recent times the idea that teachers needed to receive specific preparation to work effectively with diverse populations took hold as the education profession began to define goals and curricula for multicultural teacher education. Gay (1987) outlined three components for multicultural teacher education—knowledge, attitudes, and skills. The 1970s saw a proliferation of a number of models for multicultural teacher education in part to meet the requirements of the National Council for Accreditation of Teacher Education (NCATE). Many teacher education program models include some of the components of Gay's model (Baker, 1974; Banks, Carlos, Garcia, Gay, & Ochoa, 1976). They tend to emphasize instructional skill, knowledge acquisition—including historical knowledge and sociological knowledge about ethnic groups in America—and attitude development.

The emphasis on multicultural teacher preparation in schools and colleges of education that had some momentum in the 1970s was dislodged by the political and economic climate of the country. As teacher education enrollments plummeted in the early 1970s, and universities experienced budget cutbacks, the attention shifted to sustaining anemic and weakening teacher education programs. Discussions about multicultural teacher education shifted from positive to negative, in part because criticisms were voiced about the fragmented and superficial modifications that many teacher education programs employed to meet the NCATE requirements (Goodwin, 1997). In the 1980s *A Nation at Risk* and the reforms that followed also took the attention away from multicultural teacher education and placed it on school accountability, competency testing for students, higher standards, teacher testing on content knowledge, and so on.

Teacher educators must refocus their policies and actions regarding the role of schools and colleges of education in two areas: (1) reforming their programs to prepare teachers who will serve an increasingly ethnic/cultural minority student population and (2) increasing access to teacher preparation programs for cultural minority groups.

More than 90 percent of teachers in the United States are white. In contrast 60 percent of public school students are white, 17 percent are black, 18 percent are Hispanic, and 5 percent are Native American and other groups. The percentage of minority teachers is not expected to equal the percentages of minority students in our schools at any time in the foreseeable future. This leaves the education of what is estimated to be a national minority student population of 41 percent in the hands of white teachers. Teachers have consistently declared their concerns about their inability to reach and teach minority and low-income students. They also frequently express their frustration with their level of preparation in schools and colleges of education and, in their subsequent employment, with their professional preparation and lack of support in the challenge to successfully educate and motivate minority, low-income, second-language, and special needs students. To play a constructive role teacher educators should consider the following:

- Teacher preparation has to include an explanation of the pursuit of equal opportunity by minorities as a sociopolitical struggle within a democracy that is obligated by its commitment to equality, justice, and equal rights.
- Societal influences affecting the educational status of minority students must be recognized and accounted for in our public school instructional and assessment strategies. Both societal and school factors affect student engagement and performance in our public schools.
- Teachers must be prepared to refocus on the mission of preparing young citizens in minority communities for democratic citizenship, political participation, and service in addition to "closing the achievement gap." Democratic participation in school structures, curriculum, and extracurricular activities is essential preparation for future citizenship.
- Teachers have to be able to comfortably teach race, racism, discrimination, and ethnic conflict as well as explain avenues for national unity through democratic participation and problem resolution.

REFERENCES

Acuna, R. (1988). *Occupied America: A history of the Chicanos.* New York: Harper Collins.

Apple, M. (1996). *Cultural politics and education.* New York: Teachers College Press.

Apple, M. W., & Beane, J. A. (1995). *Democratic schools.* Alexandria, VA: Association for Supervision and Curriculum Development.

Baker, G. C. (1974). Instructional priorities in a culturally pluralistic school. *Educational Leadership, 32*(3), 176–182.

Bambritta, R., Milne, R. A., & Davis, R. (1991). *The politics of unequal educational opportunity.* New York: Doubleday.

Banks, J. (1997). *Educating citizens in a multicultural society.* New York: Teachers College Press.

Banks, J. A., Carlos, E. C., Garcia, R. L., Gay, G., & Ochoa, A. S. (1976). *Curriculum guidelines for multiethnic education.* Arlington, VA: National Council for the Social Studies.

Barber, B. (1998). *A passion for democracy: American essays.* Princeton, NJ: Princeton University Press.

Berliner, D., & Biddle, B. (1995). *The manufactured crisis: Myths, fraud and the attack on public schools.* Reading, MA: Addison-Wesley.

Darling-Hammond, L., & McLaughlin, M. B. (1995). Policies that support professional development in an era of reform. *Phi Delta Kappan, 76*(1), 1–15.

Dewey, J. (1913). Education from a social perspective. In J. A. Boydston (Ed.), *John Dewey: The Middle Works, 1899–1924.* Vol. 7 (pp. 113–127). Carbondale: Southern Illinois University Press.

Fuller, B., & Elmore, R. (Eds.). (1996). *Who chooses? Who loses?: Culture, institutions and the unequal effects of school choice.* New York: Teachers College Press.

Gay, G. (1988). Designing relevant curricula for diverse learners. *Education and Urban Society, 20,* 327–340.

Goodlad, J. (1997). *In praise of education.* New York: Teachers College Press.

Goodlad, J., & McMannon, T. (Eds.). (1997). *The public purpose of education and schooling.* San Francisco: Jossey-Bass.

Goodwin, A. L. (1997). Historical and contemporary perspectives on multicultural teacher education: Past lessons, new directions. In J. King, E. R. Hollins & W. C. Hayman (Eds.), *Preparing teachers for cultural diversity* (pp. 5–22). New York: Teachers College Press.

Hatcher, R. (1996). Market relationships and the management of teachers. *British Journal of Sociology of Education, 15*(1), 41–62.

Hirsh, E. D., Jr. (1996). *The schools we need and why we don't have them.* New York: Doubleday.

Howe, K. (1997). *Understanding equal educational opportunity: Social justice, democracy and schooling.* New York: Teachers College Press.

Kirst, M. (1984). *Who controls our schools: American values in conflict.* New York: Freeman and Co.

Kozol, J. (1991). *Savage inequalities.* New York: Basic Books.

Lasch, C. (1995). *The revolt of the elites and the betrayal of democracy.* New York: W. W. Norton.

Levine, L. (1996). *The opening of the American mind: Canons, culture and history.* Boston: Beacon Press.

Meier, D. (1995). *The power of their ideas: Lessons for America from a public school in Harlem.* Boston: Beacon Press.

Mitchell, B., & Salisbury, R. E. (1996). *Multicultural education: An international guide to research, policies and programs.* Westport, CT: Greenwood Press.

National Center for Education Statistics. (2004). *The condition of education 2004: Learner outcomes* (p. 49–50). Washington, DC.

National Coalition of Advocates for Students. (1992, March 25). World class standards are a hoax without a new bill of rights for U.S. children. *Education Week*, pp. 36–37.

National Commission on Excellence in Education. (1983). *A nation at risk: The imperative for educational reform.* Washington, DC: U.S. Government Printing Office.

Nieto, S. (1996). *Affirming diversity: The sociopolitical context of multicultural education* (2nd ed.). White Plains, NY: Longman.

Office of the Washington Superintendent of Public Instruction. (1998). *Percentage of subgroups meeting the reading, mathematics, writing and listening standards.* Olympia, WA.

Oakes, J. (1996). Two cities' tracking and within school segregation. In E. Condliffe-Lageman & L. Miller (Eds.), *Brown v. Board of Education: The challenge for today's schools* (pp. 107–115). New York: Teachers College Press.

Oakes, J., & Stuart-Wells, A. (1998, March). Detracking for high student achievement. *Educational Leadership*, 28–38.

Ochoa, A., & Espinoza, R. (1996). Beyond educational reform: Public equity and critical pedagogy. In C. E. Walsh (Ed.), *Education reform and social change: Multicultural voices, struggles, and visions* (pp. 179–299). Mahwah, NJ: Erlbaum.

Parsley, J. (1997, Fall). A perspective on standards based educational reform. *School Information and Research Services: Management Information, 17.*

Ravitch, D., & Finn, C. (1987). *What do our 17-year olds know: A report on the first National Assessment of History and Literature.* Harper Row: New York.

Reed, R. (1996). *Active Faith: How Christians are changing the soul of active politics.* New York: Free Press.

Ross, E. W. (1998). Educating and organizing for a democratic society. *Theory and Research in Social Education, 26*(3), 324–343.

Shields, P. (1995). Engaging children of diverse backgrounds. In M. S. Knapp, *Teaching for meaning in high poverty classrooms.* New York: Teachers College Press.

Sigel, R., & Hoskin, M. (1991). *Education for democratic citizenship: A challenge for multi-ethnic democracies.* Mahwah, NJ: Erlbaum.

Sleeter, C. E., & Grant, C. (1994). *Making choices for multicultural education: Five approaches to race, class, and gender.* Englewood Cliffs, NJ: Prentice Hall.

Spring, J. (1997). *Political agendas for education.* Mahwah, NJ: Erlbaum.

Tyack, D., & Hansot, E. (1982). *Managers of virtue: Public school leadership in America 1820–1980.* New York: Basic Books.

Webster, Y. (1997). *Against the multicultural agenda: A critical thinking alternative.* Westport, CT: Praeger.

Whitty, G., Power, S., & Halpin, D. (1998). *Devolution and choice in education: The school the state and the market.* Bristol, UK: Open University Press.

Witte, J. F. (1996). Who benefits from the Milwaukee choice program. In B. Fuller & R. Elmore, *Who chooses, Who looses? Culture, institutions and unequal effects of school choice* (pp. 118–137). New York: Teachers College Press.

Wood, G. (1995). The institute for democracy in education: Supporting democratic teachers. In J. M. Novak (Ed.), *Democratic teacher education* (pp. 11–20). Albany, NY: SUNY Press.

5

European and American Influences on Democratic Practice at the Professional Development School

Postbaccalaureate Students in Early Field Experience

Caroline R. Pryor, Southern Illinois University Edwardsville

THE GOAL OF EDUCATION AND THE ROLE OF THE TEACHER

Aligning a teacher's role with the goal of education creates a need to explore the sociopolitical nature of American society. When we ask for descriptions of teachers' decisions and practices, we ask that they align their practice with their vision of the goals of education. We also ask if teachers have defined for themselves a vision of society, particularly a democratic society. We are expecting teachers to define their vision of democratic practice. Thus, the question for teachers in training and those responsible for the educational experiences of this training should be, What is the goal of education in a democratic society? Given that the United States has defined various visions of democracy, this chapter begins to address historical derivations of democratic thought and the application of this thought in one teacher training program. *Central* to this training is teachers' involvement in their own experiences in learning about schools, with school-based practice teaching serving as a cornerstone or benchmark for exemplary training. We should ask in this discourse, Does the opportunity exist for teacher candidates to reflect on their training, and, if so, do they also reflect on their practice?

If we reply that several types of opportunities for reflection exist, we should ask as well, *"Are those opportunities supported and promoted with independence of thought?"*

The Apprentice Teacher Program at the Professional Development School (PDS), developed by Scales teachers and professors at Arizona State University, might respond to the need to include practice in thinking about practice in teacher education (Zeichner & Tabachnick, 1981; Zeichner, 1983; Zeichner & Liston, 1987; see also Pinar, 1989; Pinar & Grumet, 1976; Wactler, 1990) and, in so doing, create the independence and freedom so valued by the forefathers of this country. For without independence, without opportunity for independence of thought, *the wheel in the head* (Spring, 1994) or the idealism of the majority might rise as normative (Walker and Soltis, 1992), and the independence of teacher candidates for their own interpretation of democracy might be at risk. Supporting this position is the historical premise upon which a democratic nation bases its need for public schools, the crusade against ignorance. Thomas Jefferson, credited with arguing for this crusade, wrote,

> Preach, my dear Sir, a crusade against ignorance; establish and improve the law for educating the common people. Let our countrymen know that the people alone can protect us against these evils, and that the tax which will be paid for this purpose is not more than the thousandth part of what will be paid to kings, priests, and nobles who will rise up among us if we leave the people in ignorance. (Ravitch, 1983, p. xi)

For teacher educators, a selected review of influences on democratic practice is a precursor to justifying the need for democracy in teacher training. In other words, seeking the historical premise for independence can justify why teacher education programs should include reflection as part of an on-site teacher training experience.

VISIONS OF DEMOCRACY

Among the influences upon whom Jefferson could draw as he argued for opportunity in education, Rousseau, John Locke, Thomas Paine, and de Tocqueville each suggested a confluence of the paradox of social integration versus the freedom of will. Each contributed to the argument for a social contract committed to emancipation, and each suggested that it is in the best interest of democracy that a populace be well educated. To understand the dearness of their mission, one first needs to encounter several perspectives on the notion of democracy itself. In part, the concept of democracy encompasses fairness and freedom (Ravitch, 1983, 1992). All of the authors named above shed light on these notions by drawing a substantial portion of their proposals from the anthropological understanding of social order, particularly the individual's role in an organization (Feinberg & Soltis, 1992).

As described earlier (Wactler, Stamm, Freeman, & Maldonado, 1996), Arizona State University postbaccalaureate teacher candidates enrolled in the Apprentice Teacher Program (ATP) at Scales Professional Development School participated in field experiences from day one of their program. As beginning practitioners they questioned the process of schooling partly because of their early immersion in the classroom. They had many questions about the applicability of the methods courses taught on site, about theories presented in these methods classes, and indeed about their own role as future teachers. In short, the apprentices at Scales were thinking about the goal of education. At first glance, it is possible to utilize the paradigms of Fenstermacher & Soltis (1992) and Feinberg & Soltis (1992) to categorize teaching roles as either executive, therapist, or liberationist. The first position views the role of the teacher as classroom manager, the second describes the role of the teacher as facilitator of learning, and the liberationist teacher views his or her role with a content focus, intending an emancipatory outcome of knowledgeable citizenry (Fenstermacher & Soltis, 1992; Feinberg & Soltis, 1992).

Shared beliefs. The Apprentice Teacher Program is grounded in a number of beliefs shared among most or all of the members of the task force of six teachers and four professors who codesigned it. First and foremost, this group believes that teachers should have a strong voice in the design and delivery of teacher education programs. This position is consistent with calls for greater teacher involvement expressed by Darling-Hammond (1993) and Goodlad (1997). Meaningful classroom engagement (Guyton & McIntyre, 1990; Selke, 1997) as well as reflection for democratic practice was highly regarded. The response by the task force was to include practice in thinking about practice in the experience of the ATP teachers (Zeichner & Tabachnick, 1981; Zeichner, 1983; Zeichner & Liston, 1987; see also Pinar, 1989; Pinar & Grumet, 1976), and thereby create the independence and freedom so valued by the forefathers of this country.

Opportunity for reflection. One reconfiguration of the early field experience is the systematic emphasis on reflection. Consistent with literature calls advanced by Schon (1987), Zeichner & Liston (1987), and others, this

PDS program blends journaling activities with on-site methods courses. Professors add focus to critical issues in education each Friday afternoon, and students respond by writing in their journals for at least an hour, three times a week. Students articulate their philosophy of education in meetings with their campus facilitator, university supervisor, and mentor teacher, an activity long held valuable to the on-site experience by critical theorists such as Fenstermacher and Soltis (1992) and Spring (1994). Thus, as students approach the task of thinking about democracy in practice, they have participated in a teacher education program that aligns multiple strategies for thinking about practice.

DEMOCRACY IN FIELD EXPERIENCE: A THEORETICAL CONSTRUCT

Reflective thinking. When students think about the role of education, the freedom to think through or think about their role becomes part of the self-actualizing experience of those learning to be teachers (Wactler, 1990). Thinking about teaching is documented as the conscientization of intelligent action (Dewey, 1910; see also Elbaz, 1988; Hursl, 1988) as well as a consequence of attempting to resolve problematic issues (Elbaz, 1988). In any case, student teachers think about alternatives in their approaches to teaching and, in so doing, begin to see their teaching in a broader perspective, that is, of the larger school process (Wedman, 1985). Wedman wrote that the purpose of reflection in one's approach to teaching is "to focus on needed changes, to become responsible for initiating change" (p. 41).

To become practiced in thinking about change, a student teacher needs the freedom to experience how classroom teachers know what they know. Teacher candidates want to understand how teachers make decisions about an approach to teaching (Wactler, 1990). Wedman (1985) wrote that reflection enables the teacher to "become more knowledgeable of rationales underlying curriculum, teaching behaviors, classroom management, and the social/political issues embedded in teaching" (p. 24). Inevitably, the link between existing structure and individual articulation of intentionality can create, as Smyth (1989) suggested, an awareness of philosophy and a beginning of the practitioner's claim to extraordinary knowledge.

Schools of education might turn to the writing of John Dewey as we begin to understand how personal knowledge allows for freedom and a construct of democracy in the training of teachers. For example, if teacher candidates begin to observe a mentor (cooperating) teacher as an executive (Feinberg & Soltis, 1992), they might try out techniques of classroom management that model or simulate that teacher's technique. It is also possible that the mentor teacher would request, require, or even coach techniques that emulate those they have found successful in their own practice (Enz, Cook & Weber, 1994). In deciding to approach teaching as an executive, for example, student teachers must construct for themselves an approach that appears fair, practiced, and indeed part of their skill base or repertoire (Wactler, 1997).

John Dewey is cited as one proponent of democracy in education due primarily to his encouragement of an individual's exploration or discovery of what becomes known (or is owned) in his or her own practice. To become practiced at teaching might require more than the model the cooperating (mentor) teacher provides; it might require reflection on the student's experience of the whole school. For teacher candidates to have an active part in thinking about teaching, democracy as experience is paramount. Wactler's (1990) report indicates that a thorough review of Dewey's theories of individual participation in developing and contributing to one's own approaches to teaching may be the pedagogical encouragement of freedom of thought—or the democratization of teacher education. Dewey's call is for activism in thinking about one's teaching (Dewey, 1910).

Reflection, democracy, and the field experience. Reflection in professional practice appears to incompletely resolve the issue of how to decide on a response in a problematic area (Armaline & Hoover, 1989). Dewey (1933) wrote that reflection requires empowerment of action, and Armaline and Hoover additionally emphasized that without this empowerment of action, the beliefs of the student teacher are often disregarded. It might be that for a teacher candidate, the field experience provides part of the opportunity for beliefs to become validated.

Zeichner (1983) wrote that beliefs may become part of consciousness during field experience. Action derived from experience fosters this consciousness (Dewey, 1933). The consciousness becomes empowering as reflection is the interpretation of experience. In the case of field experience, the interpretation might be by the student teacher, the university supervisor, the cooperating teacher, or the administrator (Garman, 1986). The empowerment of critique is in "the cleaner understandings, developed skills, and improved ethics of intellectual freedom" allowed by reflection (Armaline & Hoover, 1989, p. 56). Armaline and Hoover questioned how student teachers could make sense of student teaching in light of their previously held beliefs. They wrote, "These beliefs are the normative structures of the classroom teacher. . . . [F]ield experience without thoughtful consideration is ideology, reproductive conduct. It is antithetical to empowerment" (p. 47).

It might be that reflection allows student teachers to view ideology for the purpose of linking events and experiences and reflecting on how dominant ideologies limit them to the possibilities that are contained by and consistent with the ideology (Wactler, 1990). Armaline and Hoover (1989) insist that empowerment of the classroom teacher goes beyond the interpretive lens and is catalyzed into a process of thinking and understanding the knowledge with which we think.

Spring (1994) provides an example of how Dewey conceptualizes ultimate truth by relating Dewey's description of why arithmetic was developed. Spring wrote that for Dewey, arithmetic was "not derived from some ideal form but was created through social interaction" (p. 23). More indicative of both the concept of knowing (truth making) and democracy is Spring's discussion of the difference between Socratic knowing and democratic (or Deweyian) knowing. Spring's example follows:

> In the Socratic dialog Meno, the young boy learned the diagonal of the square by being asked a series of questions. The assumption is that truth is in the individual and that to see it only requires turning the eyes in that direction. In the Dewey school, however, learning to count is tied to a concrete social situation. Young children are asked to set the table for a mid-morning snack. In order to do this, the children have to count the number of students and then the number of spoons to be placed on the table. In the process, students learn that counting originated out of social necessity and that it serves a socially useful function. (1994, p. 23)

To understand how the Apprentice Teacher Program teacher candidates in Arizona State University's Professional Development School *understand arithmetic,* it is necessary to describe their metaphor, for example, their experiences of counting the students, and then the numbers of spoons to be placed on the table. Dewey postulates that experience serves the learner and arbitrates and encourages the self to create knowledge. This is known as the social focus or social nature of knowledge. This social focus, Dewey wrote, is purposeful as it spearheads or promotes the concept that society is maintained by the interdependence of participants. Separation between thought and action fragments the power of workers, and the workers become an appendage of their work or life experience (Spring, 1994). If labor is separated from those who make decisions about their work, Dewey wrote in *Democracy and Education* (as cited in Spring, 1994), the fragmentation results in a class distinction. *It is clear that Dewey was proposing an alliance between theory and practice* (Spring, 1994).

Dewey's supposition is that applied theory allows a construction (and reconstruction) of knowledge for the purpose of advancing civilization (Spring, 1994). To describe the potential for experience to be democratic, both student teachers and classroom teachers in the ATP at Scales were interviewed, and their responses became the basis for determining which, if any, of the reported practices in this teacher education program could claim alignment with democratic process.

THEORY WITH PRACTICE:
SCALES PROFESSIONAL DEVELOPMENT SCHOOL

In an earlier paper, Wactler, Stamm, Freeman, & Maldonado (1996) described the field experience configuration in the Apprentice Teacher Program (ATP) as a "clear break from the theory into practice paradigm" (p. 5). The paper described a program design that included ATP students spending half or full days in classrooms from day one of their program. The shared belief of the ATP committee members was that ATP students would be able to experience the "field" of teaching by linking theory with practice. As a test of the dynamic of the interaction between theory and practice, and perhaps Dewey's call for interdependence, the ATP students found that they relied on each other as cohort members and questioned and learned with each other and others.

Methodology. Questionnaires were distributed to student teachers of cohort 3 and all the classroom teachers and special area teachers. Teachers and student teachers received the same set of interview questions, which consisted of five items. The questionnaire was written by one professor and reviewed by two ATP teachers, all members of the Scales Research Team. The questionnaires were distributed in advance so that all participants would have time to carefully consider their responses to each question. Participants wrote their responses to each question, which were then summarized and collated. The analysis resulted in derived themes that serve as the primary source of data for the narrative that follows.

ELEMENTS OF DEMOCRACY IN
LEARNING TO TEACH: THE ATP PROGRAM

Journaling. Students in the ATP program were given time from day one of their program to write in daily reflection logs. Students in cohort 3, in the student teaching phase of their program, overwhelmingly reported that they found the opportunity to write in a reflective journal a method that encouraged freedom to think about their own teaching.

One of the questions posed for the student teachers centered on activities that allowed for such freedom: "Some of the practices and activities at Scales support opportunities to reflect on or think about one's own teaching. Describe some of the activities that have allowed you the freedom to think about your teaching." Nine of the twelve students who responded to this question expressed enthusiastic support for journaling methods. For example, "The daily reflection time we were allowed at the very beginning of the program was great," and "We have also been guided into the habit of journal writing. This writing is private and does not have to be lesson specific."

The students' responses varied when they described how they preferred to organize journaling and reflecting time within the program day. For example, one student wrote that the students would have preferred some specific time during their school day set aside for the activity of journal writing. Others stated that they also needed more reflection time, but did not specify that the time should be spent in writing in a journal. One student wrote, "I would allow specific time for weekly reflection in the day instead of on my own during student teaching. It is hard to do it on my own time." (p. 9)

Besides the programmatic configuration of journaling, students also considered types of journaling activities in their freedom to think about their own teaching. For example, some students preferred the privacy of personal reflections to the more open-ended writing that was read by their supervisors or discussed with their mentor teachers. One student even suggested that the journal writing become more expansive and include a form of dialogue journaling. This student stated, "Student teacher and mentor journal back and forth and mentor teacher writes thought provoking questions that inspire growth." (p. 9)

Support group meetings. A second practice in learning to think about approaches to teaching was the effort at Scales to implement support group meetings for student teachers. Students found that these meetings acted as an outlet for reflecting on problems as well as a time to question some of the practices they observed. The overwhelming response to the previous question (activities that allowed them the freedom to think about their teaching) was that students who engaged in conversations in a support group were both stimulated and challenged by thinking about how to teach. Some responses to the question regarding these activities follow:

- As a student teacher we have support group meetings and weekly reflections as part of our student teacher requirements.
- The support group meetings were beneficial for reflection.
- Weekly support meetings for cohort group. Lots of opportunity prior to student teaching for group discussion.

Other elements of the program that students named as "supporting opportunity to reflect on or think about one's own teaching" (first question) appeared to include the opportunity to meet with and reflect with their mentor teachers. In some cases, meeting with their mentor teachers was referred to as "discussions," and the responses indicated that the discussions centered on reflecting on practice (as in approaches to teaching). However, for one student, discussion meant that the mentor teacher was task specific and addressed the area of lesson planning, and through such a venue they discussed approaches to teaching. This student wrote:

My mentor teacher and I have devised a post lesson reflection procedure where I answer a series of questions regarding the lesson. This specific information is written on the lesson plan for future reference. Three specific questions are: What have students learned? How do I know? And what life connection was made?

It appears that both the opportunity to reflect on teaching and self-selected approaches to teaching are encouraged by formal and informal practice. Additional responses to the first question regarding activities that promoted opportunity to reflect were a weekly reflection log (formal written response to an event on campus), progress reports (weekly checklist or status ranking current teaching abilities), and close relationships outside the PDS environment.

MENTORING: THE CLASSROOM TEACHER'S PERSPECTIVE

As discussed above, student teachers found that the opportunity to meet and reflect with their mentor teachers was an inviting method of dialoguing about possible approaches to teaching. The mentor teachers also reported that these meetings were supportive, both to the students (their perspective) and to themselves as teachers and mentors. A mentor teacher who was also a coteacher in a methods course reported that coteaching graduate courses with ASU faculty was a positive activity (question 1, activities that have allowed students the freedom to think about their teaching). However, for a mentor, the reflection process can become philosophical and the analyzation overt. One teacher wrote:

> Being very involved with graduate education students—when I do something
> *I try to tell them why*—[emphasis added]—if I don't tell them why they sometimes ask, so I find myself continually analyzing why I do what I do. (p. 10)

Another teacher named the specific areas they reflected upon, both as teacher and as mentor: "Being a *mentor*: Makes me think daily about the how and why of my *beliefs*, presentations. Values."

TIME AND STRUCTURE

Another question in the interview schedule asked students how they would revise the practice of freedom to think about teaching. "How would you change or add to these activities or experiences?" Students' replies centered on the programmatic, that is, time to reflect during the day, additional time for reflection, and structured time to reflect with the mentor teacher. An interesting finding about how certified and experienced teachers respond to this same question about how they would change or add to these activities or experiences centered, as did the student teacher responses, on time. One mentor teacher wrote, "Time for teachers to relax and talk." Thus, when asked about the opportunity to think about teaching, either their own teaching or that of their students, mentor teachers replied that openness, rather than structure, was critical—for example, the free exchange of ideas, practices, philosophies, less structure at meetings.

Another question regarded the structure of experiences. The aim of this question was to find out if student or mentor experience was driven (instructed) by or facilitated externally by other experts, or if the participants were restricted in their opportunity to reflect on teaching: "What direction were you given to activate or complete these activities?" (p. 11) A few student teachers responded by describing a class session they attended on journaling and the value of journaling, where they received instruction on the elements in lesson reflection and were given suggestions for reflection from the experience of prior cohorts. Mentor teachers felt they had received support in "trying new things" but were given direction in what and when to teach, specifically regarding writing reflections about grades and attainment scores. One teacher wrote, "I was invited to try new things that's the atmosphere here—I was invited to co-teach a course, and it is a given that anyone here will work with [ASU] students." (p. 11)

COLLABORATION

Both student teachers and mentor teachers could identify many activities that were collaborative. Both groups of teachers could also identify those activities that they preferred. Thus, mentor teachers considered their practice and identified areas such as meetings (informal with other teachers, and formal, as in staff meetings), discussions, and curriculum development as areas of collaboration about approaches to teaching. Both student teachers and mentor teachers were asked, "Which of these practices or activities (refer to the first question) were collaborative with other people, and which were not?" Mentors identified practices and activities about freedom to think about one's teaching, including using the third person in written responses, which provided a collaborative tone to the response. One teacher wrote,

> I believe that we have more freedom than most teachers have. We are able to choose our units to fit our grade levels and the D. A. P. Requirements. . . . The post-bac program allows you time to reflect on your own teaching if you have been a student teacher. You can see this when you observe the student teacher and the students. (p. 12)

Other mentor teachers recognized, as did some of the student teachers, that overt structure at large meetings can reduce the opportunity for freedom of thought. One teacher, responding to ideas of freedom and collaboration, wrote, "structure at meetings limit discussion." Student teachers were less likely than mentor teachers to critique the format of large group meetings, and responded to question 3 by listing multiple activities and then listing those activities that they preferred, with group meeting found to be a positive for student reflection.

- "I preferred the support group meetings."
- "Journal writing turned into discussion which was very helpful."
- "Opportunities for group discussion, with suggestions strongly [given] by instructors and facilitators." (p. 12)

IMPLICATIONS

As colleges of education review possibilities for student teachers to reflect on their approaches to teaching, site-based reflection opportunities might be one consideration for democratic practice. In part, site-based reflection allows for classroom observation and participation to be linked to theoretical options and eventual student decision making. Giving students the opportunity to describe their approaches to teaching can be a precursor to practice that is couched in ontology as expertise (Wactler, 1990). For example, when Freire (1970) writes about a teacher's belief that reality is a closed order, static in construct, he reasons that the resulting framework is that knowledge is also part of that closed order. To reflect on and actively think about a belief is of educative value to teachers (Dewey, 1910), as it may be argued that reflection tied to thinking about teaching becomes independent of routine practice (Wedman, 1985) and possibly independent of a closed order.

Several practices at the Arizona State University/Scales Professional Development School teacher education program have been identified as supportive of the opportunity for reflection on approaches to teaching. In part, student teachers have reported that journal writing, support groups, and collaboration with mentors have provided them with an opportunity to think about their teaching. However, as practitioners in a field-based program, they have the unique opportunity to teach and reflect on-site. They can utilize the classroom as a window to decision making at a time when they can ask appropriate questions or decide to act on inner-felt approaches.

The implications of site-based reflection, however, can appear somewhat distant from the experience of the larger arena of classroom students experience; for example, how free or independent are children to think about their own learning? In part several implications for student teacher learning should occur in a site-based program. First, given the call for self-actualization in teacher education and the emancipatory potential of knowledge construction, it might be fair to conclude that the need for reflection is both democratic and directive (O'Laughlin & Campbell, 1988; Wedman, 1985). A review of the methods courses taught on-site might require a more focused use of reflection for purposeful, focused democracy.

Several practices currently identified in the ATP program, journaling and support meetings, could be replicated by student teachers as part of their practice with students. For example, student teachers could introduce the practice of journal writing in the classroom. They could utilize dialogue journals to help students reflect on their own learning. They could create pairs or triads of journaling, such as student teacher and student teacher, or student teacher/mentor/facilitator (of methods courses) and university professors. The objective of reflection is the opportunity to free oneself of the constructs that diminish individual freedoms and promulgate the inference of hierarchy. Using a writing format to extrapolate individual understandings supports action in democracy.

Further activities for consideration in university programs might be a series of discussions or curriculum seminars on democratic practice. In part, both student teachers and mentor teachers have reported that group discussions and support meetings have given them the opportunity to think about how others approach teaching. Utilizing texts such as Ravitch

& Thernstrom's *The Democracy Reader* (1992) or the Jonas Soltis edited series of texts such as Fentermacher and Soltis's *Approaches to Teaching* (1992), a site-based program with reflection on approaches could be built around the "case" of teaching. In other words, student teachers reading about democracy might be able, in large group discussion, to identify those elements of democratic classroom practice and read about the connection of freedom with practice.

Finally, and most importantly, student teachers as on-site practitioners could begin to adjust and monitor their practice. In part, they may begin to bring practice to a conscious level with the children in their classrooms. One implication of teacher education, long forgotten in writing about such training, is the arena of student outcome. A call for ontology, or sense making, by the participant (in this case, the student and the student teacher) is long overdue. Students in K–12 settings should be included in thinking about how a teacher approaches teaching. By including them, we align student teacher development with goals for a democratic citizenry.

REFERENCES

Armaline, W. D., & Hoover, R. L. (1989). Field experience as a vehicle for transformation: Ideology, education, and reflective practice. *Journal of Teacher Education, 40*(2), 42–48.

Darling-Hammond, L. (1993). Reframing the school reform agenda: Developing capacity for school transformation. *Phi Delta Kappan, 74,* 752–761.

Dewey, J. (1910). *How we think.* New York: D. C. Heath.

Dewey, J. (1933). *A restatement of the relation of reflective thinking to the educative process.* Lexington, MA: D. C. Heath.

Elbaz, F. (1988). Critical reflection on teaching: Insights from Freire. *Journal of Education for Teaching, 14*(2), 177–182.

Enz, B., Cook, S. J., & Weber, B. J. (1994). *Professional partnerships: The student teaching experience.* Dubuque, IA: Kendall/Hunt.

Feinberg, W., & Soltis, J. F. (1992). *School and society.* New York: Teachers College Press.

Fenstermacher, G., & Soltis, J. (1992). *Approaches to teaching.* New York: Teachers College Press.

Freire, P. (1970). *Pedagogy of the oppressed* (M. B. Ramos, Trans.). New York: Seabury Press.

Garman, N. (1986). Reflection, the heart of clinical supervision: A modern rationale for professional practice. *Journal of Teacher Curriculum and Supervision, 2*(1), 1–24.

Goodlad, J. (1997). Reprise and a look ahead. In J. Goodlad & J. T. McMannon (Eds.), *The public purpose of education and schooling.* San Francisco: Jossey-Bass.

Guyton, E., & McIntyre, J. (1990). Student teaching and school experiences. In W. R. Houston (Ed.), *Handbook of research on teacher education.* New York: Macmillan.

Hursl, D. (1988, April). *Progress and problems in becoming reflective: An ethnographic study of pre-service elementary teachers.* Paper presented at the annual meeting of the American Educational Research Association, New Orleans.

O'Laughlin, M., & Campbell, M. (1988, April). *Teacher preparation, teacher empowerment, and reflective inquiry: A critical perspective.* Paper presented at the annual meeting of the American Association of Colleges of Teacher Education, New Orleans.

Pinar, W. F. (1989). A reconceptualization of teacher education. *Journal of Teacher Education, 40*(1), 9–12.

Pinar, W., & Grumet, M. (1976). *Toward a poor curriculum.* Dubuque, IA: Kendall/Hunt.

Ravitch, D. (1983). *The troubled crusade: American education 1945–1980.* New York: Harper Row.

Ravitch, D., & Thernstrom, A. (Eds.). (1992). *The democracy reader.* New York: HarperCollins.

Schon, D. (1987). *Educating the reflective practitioner.* San Francisco: Jossey-Bass.

Selke, M. (1997). Facilitating schools-university communication: A constructivist approach to practitioner empowerment. In D. J. McIntyre & D. Byrd. (Eds.), *Preparing tomorrow's teachers: The field experience.* Thousand Oaks, CA: Corwin Press.

Smyth, J. (1989). Developing and sustaining critical reflection in teacher education. *Journal of Teacher Education, 40*(2), 2–9.

Spring, J. (1994). *Wheels in the head.* New York: McGraw-Hill.

Wactler, C. (1990). *How student teachers make sense of teaching: The derivations of an individual's educational philosophy.* Unpublished doctoral dissertation, Arizona State University, Tempe.

Wactler, C. (1997). *Mentor teacher/student teacher response to European/American influence on democratic practice: A case study of a professional development school.* Presented at the annual meeting of AERA, San Diego, CA, April 1998.

Wactler, C., Stamm, J., Freeman, D., & Maldonado, C. (1996, March). *Teachers as partners in designing a teacher education program: A case study analysis.*

Paper presented at the annual meeting of the American Educational Research Organization, New York.

Walker, D., & Soltis, J. (1986). *Curriculum and aims*. New York: Teachers College Press.

Wedman, J. M. (1985, February). *Reconceptualizing student teaching programs: A synthesis*. Paper presented at the annual meeting of the Association of Teacher Educators, Las Vegas, NV.

Zeicher, K. (1983). Alternative paradigms of teacher education. *Journal of Teacher Education, 34*(3), 3–9.

Zeichner, K., & Liston, R. (1987). Teaching student teachers to reflect. *The Harvard Educational Review, 57*(1), 23–48.

Zeichner, K. M., & Tabachnick, B. R. (1981). Are the effects of university teacher education "washed out" by school experience? *Journal of Teacher Education, 32*(3), 2–6.

Zuchert, C. (1991). Political sociology versus speculative philosophy. In K. Masugi (Ed.), *Interpreting Tocqueville's democracy in America*. Savage, MD: Rowman & Littlefield.

6

The Praxis of Democracy in Undergraduate Education

Jeffrey B. Dunbar, California University of PA

High school graduates entering college have an impressive capacity to effect democratic knowledge and action in their education. Throughout twenty years of liberal studies and teacher preparation instruction I have seen them demonstrate this capacity consistently. Academic work performed by students in one course, A Freshman Seminar: Ways of Knowing,[1] provides a case in point.

Students in the seminar chose to attend a college[2] with the stated mission to graduate as leaders prepared to better our democratic society. Therefore this seminar intentionally had a self-in-society emphasis (in this case, a liberal arts society). Also intentionally, this course was designed to free the students, within limits, to develop their individual and their group-member ways of knowing. To these ends, readings were assigned from Maya Angelou's *Wouldn't Take Nothing for My Journey Now* and Maxine Greene's *Landscapes of Learning*. One goal was to provoke these freshmen not simply to demonstrate authoritative knowledge about matters of self in society, but to demonstrate instead some degree of democratic competence. In the process, they were to experience individual intellectual growth, group-member bonding, and proactive participation in the wider academic community. Specifically, they were to develop their dispositions, knowledge, and skills to engage some tangible academic, governance, or social reality that affected their college lives, and undertake democratic action to address that reality. The vehicle designed to achieve these outcomes was a "real-life" project in which seminar members would craft collaboratively a properly researched and responsibly written freshman advising guide for the college's matriculates of the following year. Written in the students' voice, for students, this guide was to state the essential student-to-student information that would serve entering freshmen in terms of what they ought to know about the new academic society they had chosen to join. Then, through a performance assessment—an exhibition—seminar members would demonstrate the self-in-society knowledge and skills they had gained in the process of writing the guide, presenting and defending their project before an evaluation panel composed of peers, faculty, and administrators drawn from the college community.

Four weeks into this particular semester, however, the freshmen in Ways of Knowing encountered troublesome content about their newfound college: the Honor Code.[3] Following this encounter, they decided to "overthrow" the course syllabus. Instead, they chose to work on behalf of their entire institution to democratically effect equitable change in the college's Code. In effect they chose to transcend the seminar's originally modest self-in-society emphasis. The following is these undergraduates' democratic knowing and action "story," told primarily in their collective voice:[4] "Autonomous people are the ones who manage to be actively attentive to the world around and aware of what they are choosing when they confront situations in which they can perceive alternative courses of action" (Greene, 1977).

The Honor Code is a part of being a student at Allegheny College. This is something that all incoming freshmen learn the summer before uprooting all of their belongings and moving to Meadville (PA). While everyone was trying to say good-bye to their friends and family, they were mailed a copy of the Honor Code along with many other pieces of paper. Does Allegheny know if they even received or read this piece of paper? Did it allow students an opportunity to become fully aware of the significance of the code?

Assuming that the students did have a grasp on the Honor Code, Allegheny requested the reciting of the [Honor Code] pledge at the Matriculation Ceremony. Several things about this approach set the Honor Code up for a "falling out" among the intellectuals who came to this institution in order to further their education. Not everyone was present at the matriculation ceremony, and most of the students who were present were very preoccupied. This was the last time some young adults would see their family until the holidays, and still others were wondering how they would get along with their roommates and new peers. These thoughts, along with several other concerns, led students' minds everywhere but Safer Auditorium.[5] It was then time for students to declare aloud that they would uphold something that was still foreign to them. What were the implications of such a document? What was the pertinence of the Code at this school, and where did it come from?

Students, after reciting the Pledge, scheduling their classes, and beginning their assignments, had to next deal with the intricate policies of Allegheny College. The Freshman Seminar, Ways of Knowing, instructed by Jeffrey Dunbar has become an outlet for understanding the way that this institution works. The course is designed in order for students to grow to know themselves as learners, know Allegheny as a resource, and begin to plan for academic success. To accomplish the goals of the class, there were many things that the group needed to understand. Among those was the Honor Code. It was therefore arranged that an Honor Committee member [would] speak with the class one afternoon, and it was at that time that our small group of fourteen freshmen came into the scenario. Similar presentations were organized for other freshman seminars as well. However, a unified representation of the Honor Code was never portrayed; the same member did not go to all of the seminars, nor did all the members present the same information.

Furthermore, freshmen received two different messages from the upperclassmen, one of fear of the Honor Code, and one of a lackadaisical attitude toward it; our freshman seminar was initially instilled with fear concerning the Honor Code, yet upon a second meeting with both the FSAs[6] and the presenter, we were told not to worry because the Honor Code was "no big deal." Although no specific guidelines were presented or written anywhere for us to refer to, we were told that "ignorance was no excuse." We had already turned in homework and taken tests, which had many of us saying, "I wish that I would have known this before!"

"What you're supposed to do when you don't like a thing is change it. If you can't change it, change the way you think about it. Don't complain" (Angelou, 1994). Our freshman seminar did not like the way we were feeling about the Honor Code and after hearing the presentations, we were very disturbed. We felt that we were distrusted and that the Honor Code would not allow us to partake in an active learning environment. Both Maxine Greene and Maya Angelou influenced our feelings and created a need to take action. We then sat down as a class and recorded our reactions to the Honor

Code presentations, and ideas for steps toward improvement. Afterward, we read the Honor Code in its entirety and targeted the problem areas of the code and how it was portrayed to the student body. With our dissatisfaction in mind, we followed the advice of Greene and Angelou, and took action. Our class then separated into three subcommittees: history/background; mechanics; and current context. The revolution began . . .

Where these freshmen saw themselves starting a revolution, I saw them beginning to democratically take charge of their own education—in an area where they felt strongly that change was needed. I saw them begin the praxis of democracy in their own education. Maxine Greene (referencing Jean Paul Sartre and Paulo Freire) defines praxis in *Landscapes* (1977) as the kind of knowing that surpasses and transforms, that makes a difference in reality. To bring about change, Green suggests a deliberative mode, one that includes action on deliberation.

Those engaged, presumably, might be learning to transform their fears and their helplessness into indignation in the face of insufficiency. It is, I believe, when members of the public are involved in this fashion that they can take note of the real deficiencies in an institution such as a school. It is when they are initiated into a learning community and begin themselves to identify new possibilities that they find the neglect of themselves to be (in Sartre's sense) unendurable.

As the freshmen described in their draft report above, their discovery of "the neglect of themselves" began ordinarily. When the representative of the college's Honor Code Committee asked to use one of our fourth-week seminar sessions to explain the Honor Code to my advisees, I agreed. However, I stipulated that the session was to be interactive (i.e., no "talking heads," no video programs, etc.), include "real-life" examples of how the Honor Code had affected students' academic lives in years previous, and illustrate how the Code could affect my advisees in their future academic lives.

Even though each advisee had received (and some had read) the Honor Code over the summer and had "taken" the Pledge at the college's Matriculation Ceremony, the interactive session held with the Honor Committee leader was the first time they had seriously considered and understood (or misunderstood) the Code. Their observation that the Honor Code session in class "initially instilled with fear" was an understatement.

Their reactions to the particulars and the messages of the session were numerous and vociferous. For example, one advisee announced, "I'm really shocked! In my high school we were expected to do a lot of group work, to work together to learn, and I liked that. This code sounds like I have to learn all alone now!" Another remarked, "This presentation . . . left me with a feeling that the Honor Committee is out to get me. I feel that I will be shown no mercy if I so much as think about conferring with a friend—who's now my competition—on any assignment for any class."

Given these students' spontaneous outbreak of strong sentiments at this point in the seminar, there seems to me that a terrific "teachable moment" was at hand, if these students chose to grab it. Rather than help them to simply purge their upsets by using extra class time for them to air their complaints, or quell their complaints by giving them the "institutionally proper perspective" on the issues, or distract them by changing the topic to other course business, I chose to coach them. That is, I chose to urge them to clarify and inform their concerns and to consider action.

"Ok," I said, "you have three choices: you can continue to sound off, you can cease and desist, or you can do something! You've been studying Angelou and Greene—what would they urge you to do?"

One student replied, "Angelou says what you're supposed to do when you don't like a thing is change it. If you can't change it, change the way you think about it. Don't complain." Another said, "Greene says change a wrong reality democratically."

"Well then, I advise you to write down your thoughts, feelings, and questions concerning the Honor Code—now, before your immediate concerns dull and dissipate. At our next session we'll see if you can focus your collective thoughts towards some considered and coherent way to proceed."

The students talked it over, then agreed. One of them offered this suggestion as well: "Let's have another session on the Honor Code, and this time we ought to include a member of the CJB[7]—just to make sure we have the right 'take' on this code." Again, after talking it over, they all agreed.

The next seminar session, the students shared numerous quotes from each other's writings stated freely (i.e., without interruptions, questions, challenges, etc.). Each student had written so much that two seminar members offered to collect all the writings, "distill" and categorize them, and then distribute copies of the results to all seminar members, to be used for discussion at the proposed Honor Code/CJB session coming up. The results follow.[8]

RESPONSES OF LSF MEMBERS TO THE HONOR CODE

After the Honor Code presentation, the students of Freshman Seminar [Section] 33 were left with several distinct messages and feelings about the Honor Code. It should be kept in mind that there are fourteen students in the class. The responses were as follows:

1. Nine students felt as though they could not speak with other students—either to receive help with schoolwork or to brainstorm ideas—without citing them as sources. The feeling was that this policy seemed rather harsh.

   "The message I got about the Honor Code is that I should stay in my room, talk to no one, and think along a straight line of only my own original thoughts." —Anonymous

   "Allegheny, according to the code, is teaching 'Do it yourself or you are cheating.'" —Cara

2. Nine students agreed that the Honor Code limits or restricts the amount of knowledge that one can acquire as a student of Allegheny. They viewed each individual, students and professors alike, as resources of information that should not be [used]. Cooperative learning appeared to be a forbidden learning process at Allegheny.

   "Let the Honor Code protect us, not limit us. We are taking the chance of passing over a vast wealth of knowledge with this rule." —Matthew

   "College is about using all the resources a student can find to learn. If a student can teach another student what professors can't or don't have time for, more power to them." —Michelle

3. Eight students felt fearful of and paranoid about the Honor Code. They were concerned about being penalized for any and every infraction of the Code. Another general impression was that the college was working against them as students. "Someone's gonna' be looking over our shoulder all the time, making sure we do everything right. If you mess up/slip up, the Honor Committee and C.J.B. will be all over us. This creates fear instead of excitement for learning." —Anonymous

   "I feel that it is me against the whole college. I can share nothing with anyone, and if I do I will be expelled." —James

Ways of Knowing was designed so the freshmen in it would take democratic action concerning a "real-life" liberal-arts-society issue. These freshmen "stayed the course" with respect to the seminar's democratic-action goal: whether by "revolution" or otherwise, they democratically chose to reframe what they considered were harsh realities of their new society's Honor Code.

Having the democratic-action goal was one thing; deciding to teach the seminar democratically so students would achieve this and other course goals was another thing. The decision to teach democratically raises a fundamental pedagogical issue identified by Fisch, Watzlawick, Weakland, and Fisch (1974). These authors posit several questions about democratic education, each of which contrasts beliefs about the educational approach and suggests several areas of inquiry: teacher acknowledgment of the source of authority and subject matter, democratization of the role of the teacher, expertise in the value of various subjects, and concerns regarding directing versus coercing students vis-à-vis pedagogical use.

Right or wrong, but with coercion decidedly not in mind, the seminar's overall design and goals were similar to the respective course designs of several teachers at the college at the time who sought to reframe the traditional paradigm for teaching and learning. Teaching in these courses tended to focus on getting students to actively engage in learning. That is, students were to experience teaching that enabled them to develop (within the limits set by the academic culture of the traditional liberal arts institution) their capacities to actually learn (i.e., rather than simply learn about) academic content and skills—content and skills that mattered. In relation to democratic knowledge and skills, Ways of Knowing was intended to have liberal arts freshmen experience a pedagogy much like that which Maxine Greene describes in *Landscapes*:

> A new pedagogy is obviously required, one that will free persons to understand the ways in which each of them reaches out from his or her location to constitute a common continent, a common world. It might well be called a democratic pedagogy, since, in several respects, the object is to empower persons to enact democracy. (Greene, 1977, p. 214)

Whether or not the pedagogy was "new,"[9] the democratic pedagogy originally envisioned for this Ways of Knowing seminar seemed especially right and necessary for the "postrevolution" phase of this course. The freshmen had informed, clarified, and organized their strong critiques, had read the Honor Code (word for word), had identified the Code's specific problem areas, and (with their "dissatisfaction in mind") had decided to follow Angelou's and Greene's calls to action and had organized themselves into three action subcommittees. Especially from this point on in the seminar, pedagogy had to (I decided) "walk the walk" of enacting democracy.

The three action subcommittees (i.e., research and recommendation teams) that the students formed worked to identify the Code's history; to determine the Code's current problematic language, technicalities, and logistics; and to assess the current context for continuing to have (or not have) an honor code at the college. Once these teams were formed (democratically), the FSAs and I collaborated to help each team problem solve, stay on task, and do their respective work coherently.

Specifically, this seminar's "revolutionaries" were coached in methods of social science research and writing—(including the need to secure IRB approval),[10] introduced to aspects of institutional politics, instructed in change theory, trained in group work, and guided in discussions of the praxis content in the Angelou and the Greene texts. Simultaneously, parts of seminar sessions were devoted to "staffings"—sessions at which each team presented its current findings (in writing) and was helped by the seminar as a whole to fine-tune their research and reporting.

The subcommittees did their homework. Research was done using authoritative texts and articles, and content was located on the Internet. On-campus interviews were conducted with professors, and surveys were administered to peers. Comparable institutions' honor codes and cheating policies and procedures were identified, studied, and reported. In the process, subcommittee members experienced something of what it means to conduct social science research. For example, the History Subcommittee reported:[11]

Methods of Research: A trip to the library was made in which several persons working there knew nothing about the history of the Honor Code. It was stated that someone would check to see if there was any information put aside on the topic, but there was no luck. We were told to search the school newspaper from the early 1960s. We were surprised to see that such a minute amount of information existed on such an important aspect of our college. Nothing was found on Allecat[12] or the Allegheny Home Page. Therefore, a long time was spent digging through hundreds of issues of the Allegheny Campus (Student Newspaper).

Also, the subcommittees' respective surveys often yielded conflicting data that proved difficult to assess. For example, when the Current Context Subcommittee surveyed forty students (ten from each class level, freshman through senior), they found that seniors responded to four of the questions as follows:[13]

1. Have you read the Honor Code? (Yes: 2, No: 6, or Partly: 2)
2. Do you know of any cheating that goes on at Allegheny? (Yes: 0, No: 8, Don't Know: 2)
3. Do you believe that cheating is a problem at Allegheny? (Yes: 2, No: 6, Don't Know: 2)
4. Do you believe the Honor Code is an effective document? (Yes: 6, No: 4, Don't Know: 0)

During weeks eleven and twelve each team edited their data and findings and generated recommendations. Throughout this seven-week process the FSAs and I questioned and challenged the seminar members as a whole to consider, and reconsider, their resolve to achieve praxis relative to the Honor Code. Again and again they chose to proceed.

Finally, when the three subcommittees had completed their work, they found disagreement between their respective recommendations. Based on data each team had collected, both the History Subcommittee and the Mechanics Subcommittee found support for recommendations they would make to rectify the Honor Code; but the Current Context Committee found support to recommend elimination of the Code.

Discrepancies in their data and recommendations notwithstanding, the seminar participants decided to proceed. Coached to consider options for next steps, they decided to organize a conversation—a forum—for campus leaders who were in positions to effect changes in the Code. The point of the conversation, the freshmen concluded, was to inform the leaders' decision making relative to the Code and provoke them to make needed changes in the Code or eliminate it. The seminar members collectively crafted a documentation of their work, *The Spirit of the Honor Code at Allegheny College: A Draft Report Compiled by Professor Dunbar's Ways of Knowing Freshman Seminar, Fall Semester, 1996*. The *Draft* included the seminar's and subcommittees' project genesis, working history, procedures, data, findings, and numerous specific recommendations to change the Code. Seminar members disseminated the *Draft* to the campus lead-ers, who were invited to participate in the forum. Class sessions during the two seminar weeks prior to the forum were devoted largely to preparation for the forum. The *Draft* opened with the following statement, which serves as the frame of reference for the conversation.

EXECUTIVE SUMMARY

As our class has compiled the extensive research done by each commit-tee, we are prepared to make the following recommendations:

1. In order to preserve the existing document, and make it better appli-cable to the current Allegheny, some alterations should be considered:

A. Clarify the Honor Code by changing some wording and adding ex-planations to sections that could be misunderstood.

B. Students and the administration need to have the same understand-ings of the Honor Code and recognize its significance.

C. Include a section (a preface) explaining the history of the Honor Code, including when and who developed the Code as well as its initial purpose.

2. Consider abolishing the Honor Code as it is no longer a viable doc-ument in this day and age.

Our class has put a great deal of time and thought into this research. We take pride in the work that we have accomplished. We would like every-one who reads this to realize the importance and seriousness of our work. We would like our research to serve as groundwork for further exploration of the how the existing Honor Code functions at Allegheny today. From those findings, we suggest that appropriate modifications then be made in order to benefit the community.

The conversation included Honor Code Committee leaders and their new faculty advisor, the faculty chair of the CJB and a CJB student mem-ber, the dean of students, and the college's new president. The conversa-tion was held. The *Draft Report* and the recommendations it contained were discussed, challenged here, affirmed there, and explained and de-fended throughout.[14]

Anecdotal data gathered subsequent to the forum indicated clearly that the college's Honor Code had become the object of immediate serious consideration and reconsideration by campus leaders in positions to change the Code. For example, the college's new president remarked to one of the Ways of Knowing freshmen that the forum was helpful and propitious. He was about to convene a meeting of his executive staff to discuss the role and conduct of the Code at the college. Because the freshmen members had researched the Code and organized the conversation about their findings, he had a firmer understanding of the issues involved. Also, the Honor Code Committee advisor remarked how valuable it was for him, new to the position, to hear in detail the issues involved with the Code—details that he had missed as a faculty member even though he had been at the college for a number of years. Finally, the dean of students remarked about the value of having all the campus leaders assembled to have the chance to all "get on the same page, and at the same time" concerning the Honor Code.

Anecdotal data also indicated clearly that the praxis process mattered to the freshmen in Ways of Knowing. In semester-end narrative evaluations of the seminar (signatures optional), statements were made such as the following from three participants:

The most beneficial component of all, in my opinion, was the opportunity to apply all that we had learned from this course in the all-circumferencing Honor Code Project. We had to think critically, know our resources and how to find them, work in groups, research, and, finally, present our factually based arguments in a coherent manner. I feel as though "social action" will always be an integral part of my life, and I will be able to look back upon my Freshman Seminar and this project as the push that "got the ball rolling."

Learning, in this class, was a very active process because of our many group discussions. I found myself not talking as much as I thought that I would because I wanted to listen instead. There was so much information and knowledge to take from our discussions. I was able to better form my own educated opinions after listening to other people's perspectives and opinions. This has led me to become a more educated and critical thinker and learner. For our class to take the skills that we have learned here and make active use of them in our environment has been an amazing and extraordinary experience for me. For some reason, saying all of this makes the experience seem less genuine, so I am going to end this with a quote from Maxine Greene, who, by the way, I really enjoyed reading: "Autonomous people are the ones who manage to be actively attentive to the world around and aware of what they are choosing when they confront situations in which they perceive alternative courses of action."

This class has helped me to become more autonomous. I would also have to say that being a part of a group attempting to change the Honor Code has taught me that taking action and just discussing action are two very different things. I have often been involved in being heated up about something I did not agree with, but very rarely was I involved in attempting to change that something. I cannot say that I will attempt reform for everything that I disagree with, but I do think that this course will force me to think a little more about it when considering to do so.

Anecdotal data suggested that the Honor Code research, findings, and recommendations commanded interest, reflection, and meaning. However, in the process did the Ways of Knowing freshmen demonstrate the praxis of democracy in their own education?

The subsequent fall semester, September 1997, my 1996 advisees, FSAs, and I received the following e-mail message from the student leader of the Honor Committee:

I promised to send you a list of changes and updates!

1. In the last few months, the Honor Committee has worked to reach most LSFs[15] by the end of September, in an attempt to provide unified presentations with a wealth of information and helpful hints.
2. We've also been talking one on one with new faculty, to introduce the Code, answer any questions, and provide them with a direct link to the Committee, should they ever need it. Provided during these sessions are copies of the Code, guides to honest writing and a run-through of judicial proceedings from our end.
3. We've designed a one-page brochure to be distributed to faculty. Included is the Code, in its entirety, a complete list of members, advisors, and liaisons, and a short description of our goals for the year.
4. Currently in the works are poster designs for posters to be hung in each resident hall with a list of committee members and ways to contact them, should questions, concerns or cases arise.
5. It is the goal of the Committee as well to meet with each department during a faculty meeting before the end of the semester to initiate discussion about the Code and collect feedback and suggestions for further improvement.

6. Lastly, a home page for the Honor Committee is under construction. Included now: the Code, "The Guide to Honest Writing,"[16] the Honor Committee Constitution, frequently asked questions and answers, and an inspiring note. To also be included are links to other schools' codes, direct e-mail to the Committee's account via the Home Page, the step-by-step procedure to turn in a case, and sample cases and other possibilities. It's in simple stages now, but it is functional! I'll keep you updated on future changes. Because this semester is so packed already, any time not spent on cases next semester will be dedicated to making the Code more student/faculty friendly, with the help of "Ways of Knowing's" suggestions!

Thank you for your interest, and for getting the ball rolling last year! I'll be in touch.

So, after all, the freshmen in Ways of Knowing had demonstrated to a considerable degree the praxis of democracy in their own undergraduate education. In *Landscapes*, Greene asks,

What then of democracy? Dewey wrote that democracy "will have its consummation when free social inquiry is indissolubly wedded to the art of full moving communication." Free social inquiry signifies more today than the use of social scientific techniques and protocols. It entails the kind of critical reflection that is turned to our own life situations, our own realities. It entails the kind of knowing called praxis, a knowing that becomes an opening onto what has not yet been . . . a disclosure of the reality to be surpassed—surpassed because it afflicts living persons as insufficient, mutilating, and inhumane. There must be a refusal of such a reality and a gatherings of forces needed to transform.

The Ways of Knowing freshmen demonstrated that within the limits of a traditional liberal arts college culture undergraduates can—and will—do far more than gain authoritative knowledge about self-in-society matters that concern them. They prefer to—and can—develop their democratic dispositions, capacities, and performance to high degrees. Further, the Ways of Knowing undergraduates' "story" suggests strongly, I believe, that higher education faculty and administrators need to be more about the business of enabling high school graduates who enter college to develop—to the praxis level—their considerable capacity for democratic knowledge and action. This is especially true, I submit, for any institution that includes in its mission the goal of preparing leaders to better our democratic society.

NOTES

1. Ways of Knowing serves both as an advising forum and as a course of study to explore the liberal arts education. The emphasis is experiential learning. Discussions, writing, technology, and firsthand experience connect content in the liberal arts with books, visiting scholars, and cultural events, and campus professors, staff, organizations, and programs. Activities include attending evening programs in the arts, humanities, and sciences, crafting a research paper, and performing group work. Skills are developed in the areas of critical thinking, listening, speaking, and creative problem solving. Topics include the governing principles of the liberal arts, and the knowledge and skills considered essential for the liberal arts scholar. The focus is the balanced life (1996–1997 Allegheny College Catalogue).

2. Allegheny College (PA). National Liberal Arts, Tier Two, U.S. News Online, 1997.

3. The academic honor program at [the] College is designed to promote individual responsibility and integrity in academic affairs and to develop an atmosphere conducive to serious independent scholarship (1996–1997 Allegheny College Catalogue).

4. The Ways of Knowing students' collaboratively produced unpublished document, *The Spirit of the Honor Code at Allegheny College: A Draft Report Compiled by Professor Dunbar's Ways of Knowing Freshman Seminar*, Fall Semester, 1996, Introduction.

5. Site of the Matriculation Ceremony.

6. Freshmen Student Advisors: sophomores, juniors, and seniors who volunteer to aid Freshman Seminar professors and students.

7. College Judicial Board, the group that hears and decides Honor Code violation cases.

8. *Draft Report.*

9. This "new pedagogy" is not entirely new. In early childhood education, for example, the essence of this pedagogy was demonstrated by Open Education British Infant School teachers, reported in school-reform literature of the late sixties. They used their formidable authority, considerable command of content, and astute child development skills to empower young children to take increasing charge of their own learning within their learning communities. Also, for upper-

grade (and college-level) teaching, Mortimer Adler, on behalf of the Paideia Group, proposed in 1982 a sort of democratic-pedagogy paradigm: All students would learn to use their minds well and to focus on selected essential matters of [pro-social] democratic knowledge. Teachers would provide exemplary studies for all students. All would experience a balanced system of three instructional approaches: (1) Didactic—imparting necessary information, (2) Coaching—guiding students through their individual and collaborative learning and problem-solving processes, and (3) Socratic Questioning—provoking students to consider, and reconsider, the most substantive aspects and consequences of their studies, thoughts, and decisions.

10. Institutional Review Board—the college's standing committee for reviewing all research involving human subjects.

11. *Draft Report*, 3.

12. The college library's electronic card catalogue.

13. *Draft Report*.

14. Detailed notes were not taken during the forum. Suffice it to say that the Ways of Knowing freshmen held their ground when challenged. They responded competently, factually, with integrity. Most importantly, they adhered to advice offered throughout the forum's preparation stage: "Speak to your data—do not go beyond it, belittle it, or allow it to be belittled, or be distracted away from it."

15. Freshmen Seminars.

16. An unpublished instructor's resource produced annually by the college's director of the Writing Center, Beth Reynders.

REFERENCES

Angelou, M. (1994). *Wouldn't take nothing for my journey now*. New York: Bantam.

Greene, M. (1977). *Landscapes of learning*. New York: Teachers College Press.

Watzlawick, P., Weakland, J., & Fisch, R. (1974). *Change: Principles of problem formation and problem resolution*. New York: W. W. Norton.

7

The Democratic Classroom

A Model That Works

K. Fred Curtis, Baylor University

Several years ago, I began a course in curriculum and instruction by handing out a syllabus complete with goals and objectives, activities, and a calendar for the course. The course was a doctoral level seminar, and in my introductions to the class, I noted that a seminar should consist of a group of scholars conducting research on a topic of common interest, sharing that research within the group, and then disseminating the results in scholarly form. In the activity portion of the syllabus, I provided the topic that the class would study during the term. Then I launched into what was to be another traditionally taught course.

At the beginning of the next class session, a student acting as spokesperson for the rest of the class asked if I really believed my definition of seminar, a collection of scholars conducting research on a topic of common interest, sharing that research within the group, and then disseminating the results in scholarly form. My answer to his question obviously was yes, and I had structured the course to reflect that definition. However, the class met after the first session and discussed their topic of common interest, which was different from the topic I had provided them. Their topic reflected a pressing need they all shared. The State Education Agency mandated that each school district develop a plan for the identification and education of at-risk students. Most of the students in the class were public school administrators and would be involved in developing plans for their respective districts. After listening to the class discuss the topic, I asked them to draft a formal proposal defining the topic and outlining their strategies for research. Thus, my first attempt at administering a democratic classroom was born.

My students seemed to develop instant ownership of the topic and expressed a level of intensity I had not experienced before. They appointed a chairperson to assemble the group and made assignments to each member of the class. The first week was spent looking at all aspects of the at-risk population, and at the next class session, a final list of topics to be studied was developed. Each member of the class was assigned one or more of the topics to research, and time lines were established for completing the research.

The progress in the research was reported during each class meeting. As each topic was discussed by its researcher, members of the class would offer suggestions for further research or redirection of research. An interesting dynamic developed within the class. Class members were candid in their interactions with each other, and it was obvious that their expectations were very high. Interactions seemed always positive—at no time were any negative responses observed.

As the instructor for the course, my role changed dramatically. I moved from director to advisor, a role I enjoyed very much. Most of my time was spent working with individuals or small groups. Somehow, I did not seem to miss the didactic portion of the course I had always enjoyed. I even lost or at least lowered my own feeling of my exaggerated importance to the success of the project. There were times, however, when I had to "bite my tongue" if I felt a solution or result was obvious. The discovery mode in the course was alive and well, and I sensed the excitement and satisfaction that began to develop in the class.

As the research continued, the students began to discuss the dissemination of the results. It seemed that these results could and should be made available to administrators in other districts throughout the state. The class felt that the quality of research and writing was at a level that merited publishing, so they decided to proceed with it. The class met in extra sessions and developed the process for publishing and marketing their product. They decided to use desktop publishing and to print the materials themselves. They selected the ring binder format and had an attractive logo printed on the cover of the binder. They designed brochures describing the publication and completed plans to market the document.

When the document was completed, the pride the students exhibited was overwhelming. The pride they had, however, could not match the pride I had in them. These feelings were enhanced considerably after marketing of the document was completed. Five hundred copies were printed, and all were sold in districts throughout the state. Also, a number of papers were presented at state and national meetings on the process and product of the project.

All the goals and objectives for the course were met and certainly exceeded. Students took with them a feeling of the excitement of learning that could never have been equaled in a traditionally taught course. They also agreed that they had never worked as hard in any class they had taken before. In the years since this course was taught, I've talked with many of the students, and all continue to remember the course and students in the course with fondness and satisfaction.

In the years following this course, I've offered all my graduate classes the opportunity to experience this type of course. Some feel more comfortable in a traditionally taught class, while some have accepted the challenge of the more contemporary, democratic format. The results from subsequent courses have been different from the initial course, but all have resulted in similar feelings, as noted on the following four-question survey given to students at the completion of each course:

1. Would you have preferred a more traditional approach to instruction in this course? Please explain.
2. Were your personal objectives for this course met?
3. How would you change the course to make it more effective?
4. Please make comments concerning the course.

On item 1, all students responded no. They preferred this course style and said they would like more courses taught in a similar fashion. On item 2, all students responded yes. Item 3 has had varied responses. Most of the responses included the need for more time (a variable difficult to control). Many left this item blank. In responding to item 4, most of the students reinforced the course as a unique "learn by doing" approach. Most liked the reduced emphasis on lecture and enjoyed the interaction with other students and the instructor. Many felt that the course took more time. Some felt intimidated at the beginning of the course but as the course went on became more comfortable.

IN CONCLUSION

Teaching courses using democratic strategies is very satisfying, both for the student and the instructor. It's enjoyable observing students who function as active participants in their learning, and employing democratic strategies certainly requires active participation. Sitting passively in a classroom places parameters on what is learned. Democratic strategies remove these limits and allow students to move well beyond.

8

Democratic Practices in Education and Curriculum

Kay W. Terry, Western Kentucky University, and Nancy P. Gallavan, Southwest Missouri State University

As each of us approached our contributions to this chapter, we thoughtfully considered the concepts, practices, and, particularly, the contexts applicable to the words *democracy* and *democratic practices in education* as both viable and visible forces etched into the curriculum (instruction and assessment) found in pre-K–12th grade classrooms across the United States. Many different researchers have investigated these topics producing dozens of studies and a range of findings available in the other chapters of this book that delineate an array of scholarly definitions and pragmatic manifestations of these terms. Independently, each of us reflected upon our own experiences both in and out of classrooms, empowering us to clarify our abilities to define and describe "democracy" and "democratic practices" broadly, to understand their related roles, rights, and responsibilities throughout the educational enterprise, and to appreciate their purposes and power in relationship to ourselves, schools, and society. As teacher educators, we quickly transferred these insightful discoveries to our work in preparing teachers for today's classrooms.

KAY'S JOURNEYS

During the early 1990s, I traveled to China (Red China or Mainland China, as I had learned to call it as a child). I was a member of a group of educators that included public school teachers, deans of colleges of education, and everyone in between. At that time I was both a public school classroom teacher and a university doctoral candidate. Our tour group visited all sorts of historical government buildings, cultural museums, shopping areas, civic centers, educational institutions, and so on. I was amazed not only by the actual physical sites we saw; I was profoundly moved by the cultural environments and societal atmospheres that we encountered everywhere we went.

One major impression was Chinese security. Armed guards stood outside most of the places we went. As we boarded airplanes, trains, even our buses, armed guards were evident in all locales accompanying us through the expected yet continual document and luggage checkpoints. I do not recall anyone from our tour group being detained, but on several occasions I observed other travelers being detained. Our group seemed to be well prepared and fully protected throughout our trip. Not only did we have a Chinese guide and translator for in-country travel, but we were also assigned two Chinese government officials to watch us and to ensure that our trip progressed smoothly. We were told that in China, all authority figures, including the police, the army, the secret police, and so on, are part of the national security force; these are not separate entities.

My memories are filled with images of being watched everywhere we went. When we left our hotels to walk, we were followed. One member of our group was an avid jogger. The Chinese policeman assigned to follow him could not keep up with him and finally gave up. I could look out the windows of the hotel and see these security officers waiting and watching behind the trees. As we visited various locations, special tours and interviews were arranged so we could take pictures and ask questions, particularly of school and university personnel as well as some governmental officials, including the individual in charge of education in China at that time. When we wished to ask questions, frequently it seemed as if the Chinese representatives were not completely comfortable or willing to talk to us; they would look around to see who was there or who was watching our exchange. Sometimes the Chinese representative seemed to ignore our questions, and we wondered if this was their way of not addressing sensitive issues.

A few years later I visited the Soviet Union shortly before the country was divided into many smaller countries, again as a member of an educational group. I had heard all sorts of rumors about the border and airport checkpoints and expectations we should have when entering the Soviet Union. We were fortunate on this trip as all went well. But, once more, I found that there were armed guards everywhere we went. Upon our initial arrive in Moscow, we went directly to our hotel. As most of us were experiencing some jet lag, and our body clocks were confused, some members of our group decided to take a walk before going to bed. Other members of our group went to bed right away and then got up and walked in the early hours of the morning. We must have been a nightmare for the Soviet police as they also tried to follow us as we wandered. We had many of the same experiences during our travels in the Soviet Union that we had in China. As we departed the Soviet Union from what was then Leningrad, our luggage was checked again, and our airplane surrounded by armed guards.

My travels led me to realize that democracy as I knew it surely was not present in these two locations. Individuals in these countries did not enjoy the same freedoms we in the United States seem to take for granted, such as freedom of expression, freedom of the press, freedom to own firearms, freedom of movement, freedom to obtain an education, freedom to find and select one's own residency, freedom to find and select one's own employment, right to privacy, and so on.

Democratic practices definitely were not present in either the Chinese or Soviet schools, where the atmosphere reminded me of the authoritarian, controlled environments characteristic of the colonial schools. Both Chinese and Soviet classes were large; teachers were in total control and followed a national curriculum; diversity was *not* a consideration, as survival of the fittest reigned. Students wore uniforms, long days were standard, excuses were not tolerated, competition was expected, and excellence was both strived for and rewarded.

NANCY'S JOURNEYS

I, too, have been fortunate to have traveled around the world touring countries, seeing sights, and visiting with individuals both on my own and as a member of assorted educational tour groups to compare and contrast the structures, functions, and purposes of various societies and schools with those found in the United States. As with many other educators, my experiences and impressions associated with democracy parallel those expressed in the summaries of Kay's journeys.

My journeys have also taken me to many communities and schools within the United States. In some schools, I have seen exemplary manifestations of democracy and democratic practices guiding classroom learning experiences; school-wide relationships among faculty, staff, and students; and connections within the community. These illustrative models demonstrate the concepts and practices that accentuate democracy as visible and viable forces in all that is taught and all that is caught.

However, I have seen far too many schools and classrooms that do not reflect, much less guarantee, the freedoms and rights that most U.S. educators either take for granted or presume to exist ubiquitously across the nation. I have visited school districts, schools, and individual pre-K–12th grade classrooms in urban, suburban, and rural settings within every geographical region of the United States where school boards, school administrators, and classroom teachers fail to advocate democracy or incorporate democratic practices with their students. Unfortunately, many schools and classrooms still exist across the United States in the twenty-first century where authority figures dictate the academic, social, and, therefore, emotional, growth and development of their students (teachers and school community members).

Teachers who seek employment in these schools generally have little or no choice in the curriculum, instruction, assessment, and management of their environments. Frequently, teachers have elected to work in these districts and schools because there are few or no other schools within a reasonable driving distance, all of the districts' school administrators follow the same autocratic approach, or the administration has decided to follow a sweeping autocratic approach and teachers feel compelled to stay to maintain their careers with that particular district or school.

However, in many cases, it is the individual classroom teacher who creates the classroom environment and teaching/learning style, determining how to interpret broad school-wide expectations. Unfortunately, some teachers have established learning environments that tend to be teacher centered, didactic, repetitive, boring, and punitive. These environments usually lack motivation, inspiration, creativity, interaction, and satisfaction (for either the student or the teacher). More importantly, these teachers frequently communicate inequities and unfair practices that fail to promote responsive and responsible pedagogy across the curriculum (Gay, 2000). Due to a plethora of issues including, but not limited to, race, ethnicity, gender, language, geography, socioeconomic status, family configuration, religious beliefs, sexual orientation, body size, abilities, needs, interests, and so on, school administrators and classroom teachers appear to support stereotypes, biases, and discrimination evident in their words and actions generated through both formal and informal interactions. Democracy and democratic practices clearly are absent from these schools, classrooms, and particularly, the young people's foundations that will remain with them throughout their lives.

DEMOCRATIC PRACTICES IN U.S. SCHOOLS

As we have noted, schools both outside and inside the United States differ greatly in many ways. Most U.S. teacher educators agree that our goal as teacher educators is to prepare contemporary teachers to provide classroom environments that include democratic practices. To meet this challenge, we need to understand the three types of classroom governance that help form classroom environments. Dreikurs, as outlined by Riner (2000), suggests that one type is autocracy, where teachers are in full control, give orders or commands, and totally control the curriculum, including the rules and policies of the classroom. A second type is anarchy, or laissez-faire, where the teacher controls as little as possible and accepts no responsibility for what happens in the classroom. The third type is democracy, a governance system guiding classroom settings where teachers and students operate collaboratively, negotiate, compromise, and determine what will take place in the classroom through consensus, providing a "balance between order, freedom, rights, and responsibility" (p. 410).

One of the most important responsibilities of the teacher in the democratic classroom relies on the teacher's astuteness to be kind yet firm in helping all students to learn the knowledge, skills, and dispositions by which they will be able to participate fully both independently and as members of a democracy. Each student must learn that responsibilities come with freedoms and rights. Classroom meetings held regularly throughout the school year enable the teacher to empower students to become more involved and take increased ownership for both individual and shared responsibilities and discoveries.

The effectiveness of any democratic classroom is contingent on the element of care. With thoughtful deliberation, care must be introduced, modeled, and reinforced positively to teach students to value both the relationships among the individuals and the purposeful tasks established by those individuals. Care must be taken to explore the democratic values exhibited in classrooms, including equality, fairness, honesty, dignity, and cooperation (Chapin & Messick, 1996). Values such as these are necessary for teachers to use appropriate strategies for structuring a democratic teaching/learning process emphasizing care of self, others, and society. As students take on the responsibilities of democratic learning, curriculum, instruction, and assessment can move from direct to indirect student-centered explorations. Students evolve into independent, active learners, engaged in the planning, discussions, collaborations, motivation, and reward reflective of and in celebration of an environment based on democratic practices.

I (Kay Terry) propose various roles for teachers as they evolve into facilitators, guides, and counselors (rather than directors, bosses, and controllers of classrooms) who exhibit high levels of interpersonal and intrapersonal skills integral to their success as developing professionals. The types of environments and pedagogy established by such teachers call for strategies such as inquiry, group investigation, discovery, critical thinking, decision making, problem solving, project-based learning, and service learning, and so on, that honor children's thinking and equip both teachers and students to be competent, confident, and ready for such processes.

Joyce and Weil (1996) suggest several issues that must be considered and implemented when teachers use democratic practices. Time becomes a significant issue as students must use it wisely to plan and complete requirements, while teachers must monitor it conscientiously to develop and implement curriculum, instruction, and assessments mindfully and developmentally appropriate for and with each learner. The democratic process can take more time and might even be considered slow and cumbersome at first. There is also an unfounded fear in many, including teachers, parents, administrators, and even students, that this process will not be effective, that students will not be adequately prepared for state or standardized testing. Finally, classrooms infused with democratic practices require a large and varied number of resources that might or might not be available at a particular school. The organization and outlook of the school can help to determine whether democratic practices will be successful for teachers and students. In most instances, school personnel do not teach, reinforce, or use the social and intellectual processes of democracy because they have not been informed, supported, or organized to do so.

Many educators may consider democratic practices to be representative democracy, whereby a group of individuals elect a spokesperson to represent them in some way. The democratic classroom is, however, a participatory democracy where all individuals involved serve as an essential part of shared decision making, shared governance, and shared leadership. We believe that democratic classrooms work most effectively in schools and school districts where democratic practices are understood, appreciated, and evident. Therefore, we advocate that professors of teacher education and professors of educational leadership forge their efforts to help transform autocratic schools into the democratic schools and societies we want for our young learners and their teachers.

DEMOCRATIC PRACTICES FOR
CLASSROOM TEACHERS AND TEACHER EDUCATORS

To expand the research findings suggested in the literature, a group of graduate students, all practicing classroom teachers, was asked to identify and describe democratic practices applicable for other classroom teachers. Their responses were synthesized into the following suggestions:

- The teaching/learning environment (school wide and in each classroom) conveys an inviting, safe, and happy comfort zone.
- The teaching/learning environment is organized around a collaborative approach visible through regularly held school/class meetings, a democratic society (whole group or representative), and achievable classroom expectations (academic and social).
- Everyone is expected to try to get along with everyone, be honest, and use appropriate manners.
- The teaching/learning environment is a microsociety with collaboratively established rights, responsibilities, rewards, and consequences.
- Everyone participates in the planning, development, and facilitation of all teaching/learning experiences including brainstorming, environment design, norm setting, reward and consequence setting, and so on. Everyone is entitled to equal voice and vote through participation and ownership.
- All ideas are accepted and valued equally.
- Group decisions are made through consensus (when possible).

- All teaching/learning experiences address the needs, abilities, and interests of both the majority and the minority voices.
- Decisions are flexible and can be revisited.
- Successes are shared and celebrated.

This same group of practicing teachers was asked to identify and describe the process for establishing a democratic classroom. Their responses were synthesized into the following suggestions. These practicing teachers report that teachers in democratic classrooms and administrators in democratic schools should:

- Share anticipated expectations clearly and honestly with students and their families.
- Enact all the concepts and practices generated in the previous list.
- Model the process personally, professionally, and pedagogically everywhere; this means that classroom teachers, school administrators, and teacher educators must be seen, heard, and accepted as individuals, educators in general, and mentors who produce for themselves the ideas they advocate in others.
- Incorporate concepts and practices into all in-services, faculty development, and university teacher education courses (especially field experiences) as integral aspects of an effective teacher education program.

Much like all pre-K–12th grade classroom teachers, university teacher educators must accept the responsibility for using democratic practices, regardless of their content areas. Teacher education students, both preservice and practicing teachers, bring an assortment of prior experiences from their personal lives, their professional experiences, and their pedagogical philosophies. It is the responsibility of every university teacher educator to instill the motivation modeling and rationale for incorporating democratic practices into today's classrooms. This responsibility entails transforming the university classroom into one that is founded upon democracy and adheres to democratic concepts and practices.

This quest for university teacher educators requires a delicate balancing act as many preservice teachers do not experience democratic practices in the classrooms where they complete their field experiences. In my experience, many practicing teachers do not know, understand, or apply democratic practices in their classrooms, nor are they supported by their school administrators to advocate democracy. Thus, I suggest here that the university teacher educator must help students reconcile the dissonance among the messages (learning that has been acquired previously as young students), models (learning that occurs at the university), and mentors (learning that occurs on-site in classrooms). Some approaches that I have found helpful are:

- Facilitating opportunities for university students to reflect upon and describe the messages, models, and mentors accompanied by analysis of the actions and outcomes (Gallavan, Putney, & Brantley, 2002)
- Replicating various kinds of teaching/learning environments and strategies advocating multiple perspectives and multiple ways of expressing the learning appropriate for pre-K–12 classrooms in university teacher education courses
- Modeling specific teaching/learning experiences such as new and different ways of thinking about curriculum, instruction, assessment, classroom management, community building, and connecting learning beyond the classroom
- Role-playing various teaching/learning environments empowering classroom teachers to experience firsthand the language and actions helpful in using democratic practices (and redirecting nondemocratic practices)
- Providing choices in the course syllabus for investigating and expressing learning shared with all members of the learning community, including design of the calendar, meeting times, meeting places, assessments, and so on.

The more student ownership that can be built into the teaching/learning environment, the more interest and motivation will be established. Understandably, some elements of the class will always remain the prerogative and responsibility of the classroom teacher. Yet classroom teachers must find ways to incorporate participatory democracy for every student. Democracy and democratic practices in the classroom seem to create students "who are responsible, morally, intellectually and socially, for their own learning and that of their fellow students" (Ellis, 1991). Students (of all ages and at all stages) become more independent, responsible, and trustworthy. Through democracy and democratic practices in the curriculum (instruction and assessment), all teachers and teacher educators contribute to producing good citizens. By shifting our thinking and actions from concerns of command and control, we empower our students to be caring, constructive, and creative.

REFERENCES

Chapin, J. R., & Messick, R. G. (1996). *Elementary social studies: A practical guide* (3rd ed.). White Plains, NY: Longman.

Ellis, A. K. (1991). *Teaching and learning elementary social studies* (4th ed.). Boston: Allyn & Bacon.

Gallavan, N. P., Putney, L. G., & Brantley D. K. (2002). The influences of modeling: Elementary school preservice teachers rate their levels of competence and confidence for teaching social studies. *Social Studies and the Young Learner, 14*(3), 28–30.

Gay, G. (2000). *Culturally responsive teaching: Theory, research, and practice.* New York: Teachers College Press.

Joyce, B., & Weil, M. (1996). *Models of teaching* (5th ed.). Boston: Allyn & Bacon.

Oakes, J., & Lipton, M. (1999). *Teaching to change the world.* Boston: McGraw-Hill.

Riner, P. S. (2000). *Successful teaching in the elementary classroom.* Upper Saddle River, NJ: Merrill.

Short, K. G., & Harste, J. C., with Burke, C. (1996). *Creating classrooms for authors and inquirers* (2nd ed.). Portsmouth, NH: Heinemann.

Spring, J. (1994). *The American school* (3rd ed.). New York: McGraw-Hill.

Welton, D. A., & Mallan, J. T. (1996). *Children and their world: Strategies for teaching social studies* (5th ed.). Boston: Houghton Mifflin.

9

Democracy in Education

Shared Governance

Joseph N. Macaluso, Our Lady of Holy Cross College

The character of a school is based on how the school is viewed by its own membership and by outsiders in both ethical and moral terms. The challenge for leaders is to balance and make peace with the managerial and the moral competition. In discussing the moral imperative in administration, leadership values—such as purposing, empowering, outraging and kindling outrage in others, and arguing for the balance among bureaucratic, psychological, professional, and moral school authority—that lean toward professional and moral challenge should be considered. The "professional manager" (Sergiovanni, 1995, p. 315) conception of a school leader entails placing concerns for substance over concerns for process.

Zaleznik (as cited in Sergiovanni, 1995) described "the managerial mystique as the antithesis of leadership" (p. 315). The building of consensus and committing to values that are shared can be nothing more than devices for maintaining an unsatisfactory status quo and can very well discourage dissent. "Cultural leadership can provide principals with levers to manipulate others that are more powerful than the levers associated with bureaucratic and psychological authority" (Lakomski as cited in Sergiovanni, p. 316). Lakomski further states,

> To put the objection more strongly, it may be argued that if all cultural analysis does is to help those in power, such as principals and teachers, to oppress some students more effectively by learning about their views, opinions, and "student cultures," then this method is just another and more sophisticated

way to prevent students (and other oppressed groups) from democratic participation in educational affairs. (p. 316)

Cultural leadership is a way of masking the problems of diversity, justice,
and equality in schools. Cultural leadership is not democratic, and this
type of leadership could compromise democratic values. Not all
covenants are equal, and values of different school communities are not
interchangeable.

Apple and Beane (1995) cite from Dewey's *Democracy and Education*
(1916) that a democratic society "must have a type of education which
gives individuals a personal interest in social relations and control" (p. 5).
It seems to follow that when administration and staff in schools collaborate on decisions concerning the schools, the staff's commitment to purpose is increased, and, consequently, morale is improved (Hollier, 1996).

Clark and Meloy (as cited in Sergiovanni, 1995) "propose the Declara-
tion of Independence as a metaphor for managing schools to replace bureaucracy" (p. 317). This ensures that all management decisions in
schools support the values of equality, life, liberty, and the pursuit of happiness, all based on consent of those who are governed. Quantz, Cam-
bron-McCabe, and Dantley (as cited in Sergiovanni, 1995) claimed:

> that democracy implies both a process and a goal, that the two, while often
> contradictory, cannot be separated. They believe that democratic processes
> cannot justify undemocratic ends. Even though an appeal to democratic au-
> thority cannot provide a clear and unequivocal blueprint for action in every
> particular instance, it can provide a general and viable direction for intelli-
> gent and moral decision making by school administrators. (p. 317)

ETHICAL LEADERSHIP: TRUST, HONESTY, AND OPINIONS

Blase, Blase, Anderson, and Dungan (1995) described eight approaches to
democracy in education by different principals. In one of the segments,
the authors stated that in the "old" days, before shared governance, the
principal used human relations skills to create an effective school. He used
the same approach to leadership to get teachers to adopt teaching methods
that he believed in and got teachers to give up basal readers. He attended
a reading conference presentation called Success in Reading and Writing,

which used a modified whole-language program. He felt this was the program offered the best direction for his school. Upon his return from the conference, he talked with teachers about it and suggested that he would buy the manual for anyone interested in the program. One by one they all volunteered. He brought in a consultant to do an in-service session at the end of the school year. He then told his teachers they would have a choice next year of using the traditional teaching approach, or they could choose to have a Success Classroom. There was no opposition, and the teachers returning next fall wanted to implement the Success Program. Since there was no opposition, he was able to easily implement the new program.

Another point of view on this topic is when a principal comes in and says, "Well folks, I've decided we're going to have cooperative learning in every classroom and you are going to go through this great training session." Some of the faculty will do it, some might even be excited, but a lot of them will say, "I'll show you, I might have to go to that training, and I might have to watch that video, but I'm not doing any more than I want to." It is hard to get past resistance of that sort (pp. 125–126).

With democratic leadership you don't have that, for you have people who are enthusiastic and concerned about improving. In this second viewpoint, the principal is no longer the expert with all the answers who must convince teachers of a good idea but becomes a facilitator who creates a safe atmosphere for sharing ideas. He believes that shared governance requires honesty and openness. However, these qualities alone do not constitute good leadership. "You can be honest and open and be a fool, and you wouldn't be an effective learner. You got to have leadership skills and consider the good of the school" (p. 127). What constitutes shared governance and leadership has to do with facilitating, good judgment, and developing followers into leaders.

Blase, Blase, Anderson, and Dungan (1995) suggested that democratic leadership can be an answer to the stress of shouldering all the responsibility and trying to be everything to all people. This is how many principals back themselves into an unhealthy role in which they become isolated and not able to enjoy any collegiality. The principal "finds his greatest answer to be the sense of collegiality that he has developed with teachers" (p. 127). Shared governance is not only more healthy for principals and the school climate, but it is also eventually more efficient. Teachers are more likely to implement decisions that they have been involved in making.

Successful leaders know the difference between "power over" and "power to or power with." "Power over" refers to controlling people. It includes asking such questions as "how can I control people so they turn out the way I want?" It also refers to dominating, controlling, and dealing with a hierarchy that is bureaucratic. It includes wanting and needing to be in a position of dominance and control. "Power to" or "power with," however, indicates being able to facilitate—the power to be able to do something, to accomplish something, and to help others do the same.

There is far less dependence on and emphasis given to what people do, and more emphasis is put on what they accomplish (Sergiovanni, 1996, p. 135).

REFORM MOVEMENTS

One reform movement, termed legislative learning, came on the horizon in the early 1970s as part of school accountability, competency-based education, and performance contracting. It was touted as a new, scientific view in which research could uncover scientific principles and elements of effective schools and effective teaching (Glickman, 1990, p. 435). The Nation at Risk report in 1983 discussed the mediocrity of education and declared that schools have done a ruinous job to the economy and society. An unfriendly nation wishing to undermine the United States could not have done more thorough damage than we have done in our schools (Glickman, 1990, p. 435). Banner words for governors and legislative learning were "academic excellence." Therefore, legislative learning and academic excellence reflected an essentialist, top-down reform movement that viewed teachers and administrators as the problem rather than the solution to poor schools" (Glickman, 1990, p. 436).

A second reform movement that emerged more recently is "empowerment," which espouses a different experimental and pragmatic view on school reform: Local teachers and administrators are the solution, rather than the problem, in school reform. Schools need to be deregulated so as to give local educators the maximum flexibility to address the unique educational and instructional concerns of the students and community (Glickman, 1990, p. 436). This bottom-up view attempts to promote variety and not uniformity of practices across schools and districts. Glickman suggests that "best practice must be derived from what is best for students by those teachers closest to them" posing the following questions:

> Is it desirable to move from an era of legislative, top-down reform to an era of grass roots, bottom-up reform? Will shared leadership solve nagging concerns? His answer to this is more schools will improve than won't. Shared leadership will propel more schools than not into purposeful actions. More innovations will be successful than not. However, it is not Utopia. (p. 443)

In a study by Steimel (1995), school leader roles change, particularly in decision making. Leaders in Department of Defense schools were bound by Executive Order 12871, which mandated the formation of partnerships between unions and management. This resulted in teachers playing a greater and more important active role in decision making. Leaders in these schools needed to be particularly concerned about the erosion of managerial obligations and concerns as specified by their union contracts. Strategies to help administrators understand and cope with the shared decision-making process without giving up their authority were examined. Options included holding round table discussions, including teachers in decisions about noncontractual issues, and engaging in collaborative, rather than collective, bargaining procedures. The study claimed that school leaders would not lose face or ground if certain decisions related to improved conditions for students were implemented. A balance between the need to manage and the need to share ownership remains a constant challenge to these administrators (Steimel, 1995).

According to Morgan (1986), who was cited in Hanson (1996), the decision-making process energizes and directs an organization's actions. It is usually found as the target of the political environment. Organizational policies usually arise when people start thinking and acting differently. The diversity that results from thinking and acting differently usually creates tension that must be resolved through political means. There are several ways in which this can be done: autocratically (We'll do it this way"); bureaucratically ("We're supposed to do it this way"); or democratically ("How shall we do it?"). In each case the choice between alternative paths of action usually hinges on the power relations between the actors involved (Morgan, p. 148).

Weber State University in Utah, in dealing with faculty and administrators, implemented a program that shared decision making and governance between the two groups. Critical to the success of the program were communication, full faculty involvement, and mutual trust among all participants. They compared two major decisions and their outcomes. One decision was made without any input from the faculty, the other with fully shared decision making (Thompson, 1994).

AN ELEMENTARY NONPUBLIC SCHOOL SDM PROGRAM

Hollier (1996) declared that shared decision making (SDM) is a democratic management style involving all stakeholders in making school-based decisions. To introduce the process of SDM requires the restructuring of school management styles in most schools. In the process of this restructuring, the typical autocratic leadership style is replaced by a more facilitative style that invites comments and input from all stakeholders (p. 1). In 1996, Hollier did a study of twenty-five teachers, two administrators, and five nonteaching staff members in a small Catholic elementary school located in the greater New Orleans area. The enrollment of the school was 450 students. The administration, up to that time, had been of an autocratic nature, and very little input was allowed from the staff concerning major decisions. Staff morale was low, and the setting was ripe for a study of this type.

The purpose of the study was to determine the acceptance, implementation, and utilization of a shared-decision-making (SDM) process and to determine if the process could be successful in improving working conditions. The results indicated that SDM did have a positive effect on the faculty, staff, and administration. All personnel partaking in the study reported and reacted favorably to the process. Those teachers who had the slightest apprehension during the pretests definitely improved their attitudes toward SDM after the in-service implementation. The principal, who had some negative feeling toward the process, also improved his attitude after in-service and implementation. The support staff had a positive attitude throughout all tests and showed growth in acceptance and willingness to participate. All groups reported that the process could foster a sense of commitment to change and positive staff morale. The program developed a form of ownership, and personnel became more willing to accept responsibilities that came with the changes.

PROBLEMS IN TEACHER PROGRAMS AND SDM

The overall problem in the Louisiana teacher preparation programs is the number of mandated polices and directives of the legislature and the State Department of Education needed to certify a teacher. Specific course content and specific semester hours are mandated by the State Department of Education in Bulletin 746 (Louisiana Standards for State Certification of School Personnel) and Bulletin 741 (Louisiana Handbook for School Administrators).

Nationally, between 1984 and 1986, more than seven hundred laws affecting education and the teaching profession were passed. Because classroom teachers were not consulted on the forming of these mandates, teacher skepticism and lack of compliance ran deep and broad (Timer & Kirp, 1989).

Boyer (as cited in Hollier, 1986) claims that teachers and those in teacher preparation programs must be included in at least some of the decision-making processes. Empowering teachers and students to become a part of the shared-decision-making process creates an environment in which they are encouraged to interact with each other and to take a stand on important issues.

Patterson (as cited in Hollier, 1996) suggested that group decision making does not automatically mean that the whole group be present at all discussions (p. 10). As trust increases, people are more comfortable with deciding issues in small groups and are not intimidated about bringing their proposals to an entire group (Hollier, 1996).

Educators, students, and parents all need equal participation in decision making in schools. New ways need to be created to move democratic and active schools into the mainstream of practice and put antidemocratic and ordinary schools into the margins (Goodlad, as cited in Glickman, 1995). Supervisory actions used to be congruent with the higher principles of American democracy. To be successful in educational improvement, it is necessary to employ viable bottom-up and top-down initiatives that result in a clear moral center. No one is coerced into weighing what is wrong, and everyone works collaboratively toward what is right for all students. "Whatever is right or (morally good) should never, in our democracy, be justified by power or status" (Glickman, 1995, p. 578).

OVERALL USE OF SDM IN SCHOOLS

Schools across the nation are considering the implementation of decentralization and shared decision making. This implementation involves challenges those in education must face and identify. Our future teachers must be taught how to cope with these challenges. Three particular challenges must be considered:

1. Developing a clear, shared-education vision by all stakeholders
2. Developing effective decision-making and governance processes
3. Building well-functioning teams

A particular study of site-based shared decision making called the School Restructuring or SR Study emphasized the aforementioned problems. Some suggestions for improvement from the study were an increase of staff-administration interaction and dialogue, the appointment of members who are key players and who are able to stay focused on the mission of a school, and the participation in systematic training programs (Peterson, 1995).

USE IN TEACHER EDUCATION PROGRAMS

Watkins, Bean, and McDonald (1996) described the use of democracy in an elementary, preservice classroom paper the group presented at the 1996 Action in Teacher Education (ATE) Summer Workshop. The discussion centered on how to develop democratic values in an undergraduate language arts course. It was suggested that the professor collaborate with a co-operating teacher to determine specific preservice topics. Students then chose their topics based on their own interests and needs. Once the topics were chosen, small groups met to brainstorm ideas and activities, and the students created specific materials for their selected topics. Then they met with cooperating teachers to plan a minilesson from their respective thematic units. Here, students engaged in democratic dialogue and change while being in charge of their own destiny and performance. The education professor, cooperating teacher, and peers guided them through this process. Lastly, students performed a self-evaluation of their performance (p. 2).

"Dialogue, policy and practice surrounding this experience promote understanding and appreciation of the individual within the context of a

'Common Good'" (Watkins, Bean, & McDonald, p. 2–3). Students were actively involved in their own learning; therefore, learning was not viewed as just participatory. They were briefly living their profession in a way that promoted democratic ideals. As preservice teachers continue to establish their own definitions of democracy, it is hoped that they will become courageous enough to seek skills and dispositions that perpetuate democratic ideals they deem important, even crucial, to a better society (Watkins, Bean, & McDonald, 1996).

Watkins, Bean, and McDonald (1996) further describe, in an upper-level secondary education evaluation class, a procedure in which students were provided with course-driven, midlevel clinical experiences, such as forming base groups, logging activities for each day, using concept map activities, and meeting with interest groups. During the initial weeks of the course, prior to going into their field work, "the professor and students [took] part in interactive teaching, learning, and evaluation as a precursor to learning the importance of teaching and learning by democratic example" (p. 1).

Once the democratic climate and culture were suitably established, students began to familiarize themselves with the Clinical Experience Packet, which guided their entire course-driven experience. The Self-Assessment holistic rubric was discussed at this time, and students set learning goals and standards for their experience (p.1). The Packet consisted of a participation log, suggestions for professional decorum, basic activities to be discussed, seven course-driven activities, examples of quality assignments, pertinent letters, a major heading outline, paper format, and finally, a statement in which teachers documented that the work was original and not plagiarized (pp. 1–2).

Democracy needs to be viewed as a system in which excellence, fairness, and success are promoted. A service-oriented field experience, mixed with a democratic classroom environment where empowerment and self-regulation are involved, should promote the values of our society that need to be perpetuated.

USE IN EDUCATIONAL TEACHING COURSE

Berry and Sticker (1994) described an interdisciplinary course in educational administration geared to the development of team-building capabilities. This approach used knowledge bases from educational leadership and also from the guidance and counseling field. Team-building courses were developed with a combination of didactic and experiential components of education. Included were shared decision making, historical perspectives, change process and theory, school personnel roles, the acquisition of facilitating skills, and the group process theory.

The work of fifteen practitioners in education was described, and the format of the course was reviewed. Course evaluations were discussed at length, and discussions and implications showed that it was necessary and important for students in educational administration training to experience a collaborative process in a real-life setting. In this way, they were better able to understand conditions and ways of collaboration and to facilitate the process as school-based leaders in their particular and individual school settings (Berry & Sticker, 1994).

CONCLUSION

There is a significant need for teachers of educators to include in the teacher preparation programs the fundamentals of shared governance. As stated previously, with the many requirements of the various state Departments of Education, the programs will require some innovative, creative, and challenging ideas, along with much risk taking. Anytime we deal with change there are always risks. We, in education preparation programs, must be able to accommodate those changes and work with our future teachers to help them cope with whatever changes they face. Our skills, training, and experience in working with groups and change should help. We must allow students, teachers, and others involved in our programs to have some ownership and input. We need to empower them to contribute in areas where their contributions, experience, and expertise can lead to changes that education must implement. With this type of input, our educational programs should grow and meet all the necessary standards that government and communities require educators to face today. The final output will be students who are better educated and who can go out into the world of work with a greater chance of success.

REFERENCES

Apple, M. W., & Beane, J. A. (1995). *Democratic schools.* Alexandria: ASCE.

Berry, J. E., & Sticker, S. A. (1994). *Team building for better decision-making. An interdisciplinary course for educational leaders.* Paper presented at the annual meeting of the Eastern Educational Research Association, Sarasota, FL, February 9–12, 1994. (ERIC Document Reproduction Service No. ED 366 8277)

Blase, J., Blase, J., Anderson, G., & Dungan, S. (1995). *Democratic principals in action: Eight pioneers.* Thousand Oaks, CA: Corwin.

Glickman, C. D. (1990). *Supervision of instruction: A developmental approach* (2nd ed.). Boston: Allyn & Bacon.

Glickman, C. D. (1995). *Supervision of instruction: A developmental approach* (3rd ed.). Boston: Allyn & Bacon.

Hanson, E. M. (1996). *Educational administration and organization behavior.* Boston: Allyn & Bacon.

Hollier, B. (1996). *Introducing the process of shared decision-making in an elementary school.* Unpublished masters thesis.

Morgan, G. (1986). *Images of organization.* Beverly Hills, CA: Sage.

Peterson, K. D. (1995, August). Principals' skills and knowledge for shared decision making. (Report No. BBB 29595). Madison, WI: Center on Organization and Restructuring of Schools. (ERIC Document Reproduction Service No. ED 386 827)

Sergiovanni, I. J. (1995). *The principalship: A reflective practice perspective* (3rd ed.). Boston: Allyn & Bacon.

Steimel, E. L. (1995). Shared Decision Making with Collective Bargaining. (ERIC Document Reproduction Service No. ED 381 882)

Thompson, P. H. (1994, Winter). Shared leadership. *Metropolitan Universities: An International Forum, 5*(3), pp. 6170. (ERIC Document Reproduction Service No. EJ 499 520)

Timer, T. B., & Kirp, D. L. (1989). State school reform efforts in the 1980s: Lessons from the states. *Phi Delta Kappan, 71*, 504–511.

Watkins, R. M., Bean, L. C., & McDonald, L. R. (1996). *Scaffolding democratic practice: From the teacher education classroom to the real world of school.* Paper presented at the 1996 ATE Summer Workshop.

10

Teacher Preparation in School Decision Making

John A. Bucci, Rhode Island College

SHARED DECISION MAKING AND DEMOCRATIC SCHOOLS

There are ongoing arguments and numerous interpretations about how best to make decisions in organizations and institutions within a democratic society. Barber (1984), for example, in a historical review of the interpretations of democracy, summarizes five types ranging from authoritative democracy to strong democracy. Yet it seems clear that any movement toward a more democratic system of making decisions within schools should involve a greater number of stakeholders in the process.

While shared decision making has been discussed among administrators at least since the sixties (Bridges, 1967), there has been a sustained movement in the schools for only the past ten years to involve teachers, parents, and community representatives in the decision-making process (Lashaway, 1996). Site-based decision making, school-based management, shared decision making, school site councils, school improvement teams, collaborative schools, and teacher leadership are various terms and constructs that are manifestations of this movement. In describing school-based management, Bechtol and Sorenson (1993) clearly describe the principal advantage of sharing decision making as "creating ownership for those responsible for carrying out decisions, by involving them directly in the decision-making process and by trusting their abilities and judgments" (p. 36).

RATIONALE FOR SHARED DECISION MAKING

The rationale for the movement toward increased participation in school decision making draws strongly on the philosophical belief that this broadening of the decision-making process is more consistent with a democratic view of society. This philosophical belief has its roots in the work of John Dewey. Dewey argued for a school that recognizes the shared interests of all its members and "makes provision for participation of . . . all members on equal terms" (Dewey, 1916/1966, p. 99). In a shared decision-making situation the very undemocratic process of top-down decision making is replaced by one that encourages teamwork, equal status, and consensus decisions (Blase, Blase, Anderson, & Dungan, 1995). For many the issue of democratic schools is at the heart of a democratic society. Carlson (1996) emphasizes this relationship:

> There appears to be a lack of appreciation for a governance system that provides for freedom, equal voice, and responsibility. Is this in part because of our educational system's failure to provide both knowledge and experience in democratic processes? We must ask ourselves to what degree our schools are preparing citizens for a democratic society not just by word but also by deed. (p. 188)

From a more utilitarian perspective, shared decision making is viewed as a strategy that will improve the quality of school decisions and their impact on the school environment and student learning. Shared decision making is viewed as a means to facilitate school improvement (Noble, 1994). It supports the belief reflected in the private sector during the eighties and nineties that those in closest proximity to the problem, issue, or enterprise have much to contribute in the decision-making process. The common cliché is that the educators who know the needs of children best are teachers. The important role of teachers in the effort to help children reach high standards of academic learning has become a cornerstone of school reform during the past decade.

Teacher leadership is seen as essential in this effort. In shared decision making it is assumed that teachers, because of their practical understanding of the complex nature of classrooms, are in the best position to make judgments about ways to improve school achievement (Lashaway, 1996).

THE NEED TO PREPARE TEACHERS
FOR SHARED DECISION MAKING

If this trend continues, teachers can be expected to be called upon to participate in decisions to a greater extent than is currently the case. In a study of successful and unsuccessful school-based management efforts, Wohlstetter found the existence of many teacher-led teams to be an important characteristic of successful efforts (1995). This raises the issue for teacher education institutions and providers of teacher in-service education of whether teachers are being prepared for these new responsibilities. What can be done to improve the preparation of teachers for an expanded role in the school decision-making process?

SCHOOL DECISION MAKING:
AREAS OF TEACHER INVOLVEMENT

To what extent should teachers be involved in school decision making? In what areas should they be involved? While much of this is evolving and reflects the cultures and political structure of the various communities, there is growing support for more teacher involvement in the policy areas of budget, personnel, curriculum, strategic planning, and school change. Teacher involvement in decision making grows when the locus of decisions moves from the district level to the school level. In advocating school site management Bailey (1991) suggests that teachers should be involved in decisions about budget preparation, curriculum development, personnel issues, merit pay and career ladder provisions, textbook selection, discipline codes, teacher assignments, and student evaluation systems.

The commitment of school districts to empowering teachers to participate in decision making might be measured by examining what kinds of decisions really have an impact on schools. In a study of school-based decisions, Glickman (1993) divided decisions according to the impact they had on the school. He identified zero-impact, minimal-impact, core-impact, and comprehensive-impact decisions. Included in core-impact decisions were those that addressed curriculum, staff development, instructional programs, student assessment, and instructional budget. Those decisions that had comprehensive impact were school budget, hiring of personnel, deployment of personnel, and personnel evaluation. While the degree to which teachers will be involved in comprehensive-impact decisions in the future is not known, teachers should be knowledgeable and skillful enough to participate in these and core-impact decisions when the occasion arises.

KNOWLEDGE AND SKILLS NEEDED BY TEACHERS

What knowledge and skills are needed by teachers who participate in shared decision making? Teachers must first thoroughly understand what this means, see some examples of how it works, and recognize the pitfalls involved. Many articles have been written about the successes of school-based decision making, but those that identify some of the reasons for failure can be equally enlightening (e.g., Conway & Calzi, 1996). Teachers need to thoroughly understand the rationale for embarking on this course; they should be realistic about the time and energy involved; they should understand the role of the principal in the process; and they should be prepared to recognize and meet the obstacles.

Working with others in a decision-making process involves skills that teachers might need to develop or refine. Wohlstetter (1995) identified "functional and process skills" as being among the most important needed by teachers who are working in successful school-based management situations (p. 23). In a study of Delaware site-based management efforts, Noble (1994) noted the need for attention to the skills of intervention and decision making. Oswald (1995), when identifying the barriers that prevent school-based management from being implemented successfully, included a "knowledge of SBM and lack of decision making skills, communication and trust among participants" (p.2). Group processes, consensus building, and the change process itself were identified as important skill areas by Guskey and Peterson (1996).

Preservice Programs

If teacher education institutions have a vision of the teacher's life as one that involves a commitment to providing leadership for school improvement, they must make a commitment to preparing them for such roles. Rather than focusing exclusively on pedagogical skills and content knowledge, teacher preparation programs must incorporate the attitudes, behaviors, knowledge, and skills needed by teachers to function in schools committed to shared decision making. For some institutions the conceptual framework for their teacher education programs might need some revision.

How can the knowledge and skills essential to shared decision making be incorporated into preservice teacher education programs? The answer can best be described as a comprehensive and inclusive approach. Rather than trying to find the one place in the preservice curriculum to address this need, teacher education institutions should take a multifaceted approach that permeates the program. What follows are some suggestions for doing this.

Introductory Courses

In introductory or foundation courses, shared decision making and the role of teachers as decision makers should be introduced to students. This is where teacher education programs begin to define what it means for a teacher to be a professional.

Group Work

Throughout the teacher education program, opportunities for preservice teachers to work in groups and to arrive at group consensus should be provided. Since teachers will be involved in the give-and-take discussions of issues in shared-decision-making groups, they should have practice at doing this within their teacher preparation programs.

Skill Training

Wherever possible, lessons, simulations, and other instructional strategies that focus on developing communications skills, the value of considering diverse positions on issues, team-building, consensus decision making, and group problem solving should be incorporated within the curriculum. Each teacher education program must determine what skill training will be most beneficial to future teacher leaders and locate opportunities for incorporating them within the curriculum.

Unit Governance

Teacher education units that believe in the process of shared decision making should examine their governance structures to assess how well they model shared decision making among their faculty, administration, and students. Modeling of shared decision making can take place in college classrooms as well. Involving students in classroom decision making not only provides good experience for teachers in training but also demonstrates the commitment of the institution to shared decision making.

Clinical Experiences

Teacher leadership agendas should be built into clinical experiences so that student teachers and interns will observe and reflect on shared decision making in the schools to which they are assigned. Where possible, professional development schools should be used for clinical experiences because they typically have an atmosphere of collaboration. For example, Fairleigh Dickinson University has worked with regional schools to establish a Professional Development Schools Consortium that places much emphasis on teacher leadership (Forster, 1997). In selecting other schools for student teaching or intern placement, one of the criteria might be the degree to which a school demonstrates shared decision making. Discussions of the role of the teacher in school decision making should take place in student teaching seminars that accompany these clinical experiences.

Professional Development Programs

For many practicing teachers, the movement to include them in the decision-making processes of schools is one for which they are relatively unprepared. Schools that have successful shared-decision-making processes place a great deal of emphasis on professional development and knowledge and skills development (Wohlstetter, Van Kirk, Robertson, & Mohrman, 1997). They can benefit from professional development activities that might make them more effective in their roles as decision makers.

Since many of the decision-making structures involve parents and community representatives, some of the professional development strategies for teachers might also be targeted for these groups. "Effective school-site councils begin with effective training. . . . Such training should cover topics like group decision-making, conflict resolution, and building group culture. Without adequate preparation, group members are apt to assume familiar authoritarian or passive roles and to think in individualistic rather than corporate terms" (Peterson-del Mar, 1994, p. 2). In addition to process skills such as team building and conflict resolution, these school site councils have members who must become more aware and knowledgeable about educational issues. Teacher members must expand their scope of thinking so that they view the school as a whole rather than from the perspective of their individual classrooms (Gleason, Donohue, & Leader, 1996).

A common model for professional development for shared decision making is the delivery of workshops or consulting to a team or group that has already been organized for purposes of shared decision making. Professional development takes place very soon after the organization of these groups. When the composition of the team is primarily teachers and other educational professionals, workshop emphasis is primarily on those activities that increase team effectiveness and broaden the educational viewpoint of all participants. When the decision-making group has a more diverse makeup, that is, teachers, administrators, parents, community members, and students, there are additional needs of assuring a common knowledge base and an appreciation of the diversity within the group. Therefore, the workshops and consultation must be carefully handled so that all can benefit from the professional development.

There are many possible topical areas for workshops for school-based management teams or other groups committed to shared decision making. Drawn from the experiences of the author, these include creating a school vision, effective teams, team building, conflict resolution, communication skills, listening skills, decisions by consensus, reaping the benefits of team diversity, a team approach to problem solving, and a functional approach to leadership.

Often workshops for teams focus on developing a common knowledge of the school, the school district, and the community they serve. These can include an analysis and understanding of mission, curriculum, history, student information, other demographics, state requirements, and anything else that might contribute to an understanding of the contexts within which school decisions are made.

The commitment to the development of the team members must continue after the initial shared-decision-making team training. It should be part of the ongoing agenda of the team. Periodic workshops should be scheduled based on the perceived need of the team. Consultants or other in-house trainers should develop short exercises within meetings that reinforce previously learned skills and knowledge. Outside consultants, especially those who have been involved in the initial team training, should be invited to sit in on meetings and later offer feedback and advice that leads to positive growth.

CONCLUSION

Schools are more democratic when the top-down hierarchical decision-making structure is replaced by one that is more inclusive and that invites participation by all stakeholders. Teachers should support the movement in this direction and should develop the knowledge and skills as participants in this process. School systems should recognize the benefits of a decision-making process that is more democratic and should support it and commit resources to making it work. And finally, teacher education institutions must recognize that teachers are and will be educational leaders. They should evaluate how well their teacher education programs prepare teachers for this role.

REFERENCES

Bailey, K. W. J. (1991). *School-site management applied.* Lancaster, PA: Technomic Publishing Co.

Barber, B. (1984). *Strong democracy.* Berkeley: University of California Press.

Bechtol, W. M., & Sorenson, J. S. (1993). *Restructuring schooling for individual students.* Boston: Allyn & Bacon.

Blase, J., Blase, J., Anderson, G., & Dungan, S. (1995). *Democratic principals in action: Eight pioneers.* Thousand Oaks, CA: Corwin Press.

Bridges, E. M. (1967). A model for shared decision-making in the school principalship. *Educational Administration Quarterly, 3.*

Carlson, R. V. (1996). *Refraining & reform: Perspectives on organization, leadership, and school change.* White Plains, NY: Longman.

Conway, J., & Calzi, F. (1996). The dark side of shared decision making. *Educational Leadership, 53*(4), 45–49.

Dewey, J. (1966). *Democracy and education* (2nd ed.). New York: Free Press. (Original work published 1916)

Forster, E. (1997). Teacher leadership: Professional right and responsibility. *Action in Teacher Education, 19*(3), 82–94.

Gleason, S. C., Dohohue, N., & Leader, G. (1996). Boston revisits school-based management. *Educational Leadership, 53*(4), 24–27.

Glickman, C. D. (1993). *Renewing America's schools: A guide for school-based action.* San Francisco: Jossey-Bass.

Guskey, T., & Peterson, D. (1996). The road to classroom change. *Educational Leadership, 53*(4), 10–14.

Lashaway, L. (1996). The limits of shared decision-making. *ERIC Digest, Number 108.* Eugene, OR: ERIC Clearinghouse on Education Management. (ERIC Document Reproduction Service No. ED3 97467)

Noble, A. (1994). *Site-based management practices in Delaware's public schools-executive summary.* Delaware R&D Center Technical Report.

Oswald, L. (1995). School-based management. *ERIC Digest, Number 99.* Eugene, OR: ERIC Clearinghouse on Educational Management. (ERIC Document Reproduction Service No. ED3 84950)

Peterson-del Mar, D. (1994). School-site councils. *ERIC Digest, Number 89.* Eugene, OR: ERIC Clearinghouse on Education Management. (ERIC Document Reproduction Service No. ED369154)

Wohstetter, P. (1995). Getting school-based management right: What works and what doesn't. *Phi Delta Kappan, 77*(1), 22–26.

Wohstetter, P., Van Kirk, A., Robertson, P., & Mohrman, S. (1997). *Organizing for successful school-based management.* Alexandria, VA: Association for Supervision and Curriculum Development.

About the Editors

Art Pearl, currently adjunct professor of education at Washington State University–Vancouver and professor emeritus at the University of California–Santa Cruz, has long been associated with efforts to remedy education for those underserved. He was an invited speaker at the White House Conference on Teaching the Disadvantaged in 1966 and a member and chair of the National Institute for Teaching of the Disadvantaged from 1967 to 1969. He has worked in a variety of capacities—as teacher, researcher, administrator, and consultant—to help individuals and groups reach new levels of understanding through problem-solving education. When the Black Panther leader Huey Newton sought a Ph.D. at the University of California, he came to Art Pearl. He is author of numerous articles and books, including *New Careers for the Poor*, with Frank Riessman (1965), *The Atrocity of Education* (1972), *The Value of Youth*, with J. D. Grant and Ernst Wenk (1979), "Systematic and Institutional Factors in Chicano School Failure" in Richard Valencia's (ed.) *Chicano School Failure: Research and Public Policy Agendas for the 1990s* (1991, revised 2002), *The Evolution of Deficit Thinking in Educational Thought and Practice*, with Richard Valencia (1998), and *The Democratic Classroom: Theory to Guide Educational Practice*, with Tony Knight (1999).

Caroline R. Pryor is assistant professor at Southern Illinois University, Edwardsville and 2003 Wye Fellow of the Aspen Institute. She holds a B.A. in anthropology, a masters in higher and adult education, and a doctorate in secondary education. Dr. Pryor is author of six books and numerous chapters and articles regarding philosophy, curriculum, and democratic practice. She received the Best Research Paper Award from the Arizona Educational Research Organization for her work *European/American Influences on Democratic Practice: A Case of a Professional Development School*. In a career spanning twenty-five years of teaching, Dr. Pryor has worked extensively in field-based preservice programs building alliances for school reform.